T0658810

LEFTOVER
Makeovers

LEFTOVER
Makeovers
Great New Meals from Last Night's Dinner

VICTORIA SHEARER

SELLERS
PUBLISHING

Dedication

For Bob, who has made my life's journey such an incredible ride.

Published by Sellers Publishing, Inc.

Text copyright © 2010 Victoria Shearer
All rights reserved.
Author photo (back flap) copyright Bob Shearer.

Sellers Publishing, Inc.
161 John Roberts Road, South Portland, Maine 04106
For ordering information:
(800) 625-3386 toll free
Visit our Web site: www.sellerspublishing.com • E-mail: rsp@rsvp.com

ISBN: 13: 978-1-4162-0607-1

Library of Congress Control Number: 2010924370

No portion of this book may be reproduced or transmitted in any form,
or by any means, electronic or mechanical, including photographing,
recording, or by any information and storage retrieval system, without written
permission from the publisher.

10 9 8 7 6 5 4 3 2 1

Printed and bound in China.

CONTENTS

You're all familiar with those magazine makeovers, where the plain, slightly overweight woman having a bad-hair-day and sporting an ill-shapen outfit is miraculously transformed into a knockout, a virtual "10," with merely a touch of makeup, a new coif, and a slimming ensemble. Impossible!

While the above scenario may, indeed, be more fiction than fact, when it comes to food — good food — a total makeover is not impossible at all. In fact, it is easy, economical, and fun!

We all are faced with leftovers on a daily basis. The nagging question is, "What do I do with them?" Warm them up and eat them, night after night, until they are gone? Boring. Plunk them in the back of the refrigerator in a covered container until they grow a furry mold? Gross. Freeze them and forget them? Wasteful.

Many countries in the world routinely use leftovers to create new dishes, using only small portions of protein — poultry, meat, seafood — to flavor their main staple ingredients. Asian cuisines utilize rice and noodles. Mexicans elevate flour and corn tortillas to new heights. A plateful of Italian pasta welcomes most any leftover ingredient. The English use their leftovers in pies and pastries. Both Indian and Thai cooks spice up their leftovers in curries. Americans are partial to soups, salads, pizza, and sandwiches.

Inspired by the culinary expertise found around the globe, *Leftover Makeovers* shows you the way to turn last night's great dinner into a totally different, completely new meal. You'll find more than 100 recipes here for entrées and their enticing leftover makeovers. You can serve the new creations the next day or freeze them for use at a later date, when you might be pressed for time.

To help you save money, you'll find recipes to use up scraps, extras, and past-their-prime ingredients, such as egg whites, stale bread, overripe bananas, and spotty mushrooms.

Occasionally, you may not have time to stock up on fresh food items. Your freezer may be empty, your refrigerator nearly bare. *Leftover Makeovers* comes to your rescue with ideas for quick meals from staple ingredients. And to ensure that you stock these staples, at the conclusion of *Leftover Makeovers* you'll find a helpful list of innovative culinary makeover tips as well as a complete inventory of the ingredients used in the recipes in this book.

So, say goodbye to yesterday's meal. With *Leftover Makeovers* you'll no longer hear your family say, "Leftovers? Again?"

How to use this book

The core recipes throughout the book are highlighted on pages with a faint blue tint on them. Immediately following each core recipe, you will find one or more original recipes that incorporate that core recipe's leftovers into an entirely new dish. Everything you need to know — how many the core recipe serves, how much of the finished dish you'll have left over, and what delicious options are available to make next — are all grouped together for easy viewing and meal planning.

Look for the icon throughout the book to find great tips for being creative, efficient, and prepared in the kitchen.

The icon indicates that either a portion or the entire recipe can be made in advance, saving you time and energy on busy nights. Whether you want to get most of your meal prep done and refrigerate it for later or you need to pull a completed, homemade meal from the freezer, *Leftover Makeovers* offers a full range of ideas.

Dig in and enjoy!

Headliners
The Star Players

Poultry

Mexican Shredded Chicken
- Giant Baked Burrito
- Enchiladas Verde

Beer Can Chicken
- Baked Chicken Ziti
- Chicken-Spinach Quiches

Lemon-Mint Chicken Kabobs
atop Rainbow Salsa
- Rainbow Chicken Stir-Fry

Lime-Mustard Grilled
Chicken Breasts
- Cuban Chicken Salad in a
  Crispy Bread Bowl
- Chicken Barbecue Pizza

Grill-roasted Turkey with
Orange-Molasses Glaze

Oven-roasted Lemon-Herb
Turkey Breast

- Chardonnay-Alfredo Turkey
  Salad Stuffed Shells
- Turkey and Ham Cannelloni

Roast Duck with Fruited
Orange Sauce
- Faux Peking Duck
- Duck-Noodle Salad in Crusty
  Baskets

Meat

Roasted Orange-Sesame
Pork Loin
- Pork Pad Thai
- Mu Shu Lettuce Wraps

Orange-Mustard Glazed Baked
Ham with Horseradish Cream
Sauce
- Ham and Split Pea Soup
- Mini Ham Popovers
- Spinach and Ham Calzones

Grilled Peachy Pork Tenderloin
- Pork Tenderloin Medallion
  Salad with Peach Vinaigrette
  Drizzle

Chinese Roast Pork Chops
- Pork Fried Rice
- Pork Stir-Fry L'Orange
  over Crispy Noodle Cake

Aunt Rita's Tried-and-True
Two-Bean Chili
- Huevos Rancheros
- Knockoff Cincinnati Chili
- Frito Pie

Grilled Asian Sirloin Steak
- Asian Steak, Cantaloupe, and Brie Quesadillas
- Thai Beef Salad

South African Flank Steak Braai
- Beef on a Weck Sandwich
- Blue Cheese Steak Bites

Fancy Schmancy Meat Loaf with Cranberry Ketchup
- Spicy Meat Loaf–Mushroom Lasagna

Red Currant Glazed Corned Beef
- Corned Beef Hash

Herb-marinated Grill-roasted Boneless Leg of Lamb
- Middle Eastern–style Lamb Penne Pasta
- Shepherd's Pie

Fish and Seafood

Sesame Seared Yellowfin Tuna with Ponzu Sauce
- Yellowfin Tuna Tacos
- Tuna Salad Melt

Soy-Ginger Salmon Fillets Roasted on Potato Galettes
- Dilled Fish Spread Sandwiches

Grilled Marinated Swordfish
- Louise's Cantonese Fish and Vegetable Soup

Shrimp and Brie Penne
- Shrimp and Brie Penne Soup

Barbecued Jumbo Shrimp
- Grilled Shrimp Po' Boys
- Caribbean Shrimp Wraps

You Peel 'Em Shrimp with Three Dipping Sauces
- Shrimp Risotto
- Savory Shrimp Tart
- Herbed Shrimp Cakes

Mexican Shredded Chicken

My son Brian perfected this Mexican shredded chicken. Use this easy recipe as a base for Giant Baked Burrito and Enchiladas Verde.

2 rotisserie chickens, wings and legs removed
1 tablespoon olive oil
1 (24-ounce) jar chunky salsa
1 bottle beer
Tomato-based hot sauce

Shred chicken by hand, discarding skin and carcasses. Place olive oil in a large saucepan over medium-high heat and add shredded chicken. Add salsa and beer and hot sauce to taste. Add water to cover chicken. Bring to a boil, then reduce heat to low. Simmer, uncovered, stirring occasionally, until liquid reduces and only a little sauce remains, about 2 hours. Transfer to covered containers and refrigerate or freeze until needed.

Serve as a filling for tacos, atop a tossed green salad, or with a side of rice and vegetables.

You'll need 3 cups leftover shredded chicken for the Giant Baked Burrito and 3 cups for Enchiladas Verde.

Makes: 8 cups

Giant Baked Burrito

For a colorful presentation, put guacamole, sour cream, salsa, and lettuce in a four-portioned serving dish. Allow diners to serve themselves a portion of the burrito from the pizza stone and add their favorite toppings.

4 large (10-inch-diameter) flour tortillas
1 cup medium-spiced commercially prepared black bean dip, like H.T. Trader's
½ cup chopped sweet onions, like Vidalia
3 cups leftover Mexican Shredded Chicken
1 (8-ounce) package shredded taco cheese, divided
2 tomatoes, thinly sliced
1 cup guacamole
1 cup sour cream
1 cup fresh salsa
2 cups shredded lettuce

Preheat oven to 425°F. Place tortillas on a pizza stone or a large baking sheet so that half of each tortilla is on the stone and overlaps the next. Half of each tortilla (4½ inches) will extend off the edge (overlapping tortillas will form a 9-inch square).

Spread bean dip in an even layer over square of overlapping tortillas. Sprinkle onions over bean dip. Place chicken in a microwavable bowl and reheat until warmed through. Spread chicken atop bean dip and onions. Sprinkle ½ cup shredded cheese atop chicken.

Fold each extended portion of tortilla over chicken, one over the other in an overlapping pattern. Place tomato slices in three rows atop burrito. Sprinkle remaining shredded cheese evenly over burrito.

Bake for 18 minutes, until cheese has melted and the overlapping tortillas have browned slightly. Cut into 9 square portions with a large pizza cutter. Serve each portion topped with a dollop of guacamole and sour cream and a sprinkling of salsa and lettuce.

If you don't have a pizza stone and are using a baking sheet, slide burrito onto a large cutting board with a firm spatula before cutting.

Serves: 4 to 6

Enchiladas Verde

The tomatillo, or husk tomato, is a small, green cousin of the common red tomato. Native to Latin America, it adds a distinctive taste to Mexican cuisine and is loaded with vitamin C. You can find canned tomatillos in the Latin section of most supermarkets.

3 cups leftover Mexican Shredded Chicken

½ cup chopped sweet onions, like Vidalia

3 tablespoons grated Parmesan cheese

2 cups shredded cheddar-jack cheese, divided

1 (4.5-ounce) can diced green chiles

1 (13-ounce) can tomatillos, drained

¼ cup snipped fresh cilantro

¾ cup heavy whipping cream

1 large egg, beaten

¼ teaspoon salt

⅛ teaspoon black pepper

1 (16-ounce) package medium flour tortillas (eight 8-inch-diameter tortillas)

½ cup sour cream

½ cup guacamole

Chopped lettuce

Early in the day: Place shredded chicken, onions, Parmesan cheese, and I cup cheddar-jack cheese in a large bowl. Toss to mix ingredients well. Set aside.

To make the verde sauce, place chiles, tomatillos, and cilantro in a blender and pulse until pureed. Add cream, egg, salt, and pepper and blend on low speed until smooth.

Coat a 7x11-inch baking dish with vegetable cooking spray. Place 4 flour tortillas between 2 sheets of paper toweling. Microwave for 20 seconds to soften tortillas. Brush each tortilla with verde sauce. Place one-eighth chicken mixture across the lower third of each tortilla. Fold in sides and roll tightly. Place the 4 enchiladas seam-down in baking dish. Repeat this process with remaining 4 tortillas and chicken mixture.

Pour verde sauce over enchiladas. Sprinkle with remaining I cup cheddar-jack cheese. Cover baking dish with plastic wrap and aluminum foil. Refrigerate until needed.

To bake: Preheat oven to 375°F. Remove foil and plastic wrap. Place baking dish on a baking sheet. Bake for 25 to 30 minutes, until bubbly. Place 2 enchiladas on each dinner plate. Place I tablespoon sour cream and I tablespoon guacamole in a line down the center of each enchilada. Sprinkle with chopped lettuce. Serve immediately.

You also can garnish with finely diced red tomato and sliced black olives if you wish.

Serves: 4

Beer Can Chicken

These little birds stand up proudly on the grill, thanks to an ingenious, inexpensive little rack called a ChickCan. You can find the racks in the grilling section of most hardware and home improvement stores.

2 (4-pound) fryer chickens

2 (12-ounce) cans beer

2 tablespoons Penzeys Singapore Seasoning or another seasoned poultry rub

Preheat gas grill to 350 to 400°F. Place a shallow foil pan under the area upon which the chickens will cook, using gas burners in indirect method (burner off under chickens). Add a few hickory chips to the coals, if desired.

Wash chickens thoroughly and dry with paper toweling. Coat chickens with olive oil spray or brush with olive oil. Rub seasoning all over the skin of both chickens. Set aside on a large tray.

Drink one-third of the beer out of each can. (I'm not kidding! But you can pour it down the drain if you'd rather.) Place each can of beer into a ChickCan rack and place the racks on the grill. Place the cavity of each chicken atop rack and beer can, so that chickens are "standing up." (The beer bubbles up in the heat, basting the chickens from within.) Grill chickens, covered, for 1¼ to 1½ hours, until chickens are golden brown. Remove chickens from racks and place on tray. Allow them to rest for 5 to 10 minutes. Slice and serve immediately.

To store leftovers, take chicken off the bone and place in a zipper bag and refrigerate until needed. Penzeys spice company concocts a number of wonderful rubs for meat, poultry, and fish that are packaged in small, affordable plastic jars. Order online at: www.penzeys.com.

Serves: 8 or 4 with leftovers

Baked Chicken Ziti

This recipe makes two 1½-quart casseroles — one to serve tonight, one to freeze for another meal.

1 tablespoon plus 1 teaspoon coarse salt
1 pound dried ziti pasta
2 (14.5-ounce) cans petite-cut tomatoes with garlic and olive oil
2 cups diced, leftover Beer Can Chicken
1 tablespoon dried basil leaves
1 tablespoon dried oregano leaves
1 (8-ounce) package shredded mozzarella cheese
1 cup evaporated milk
1 teaspoon garlic paste or minced garlic
½ teaspoon crushed red pepper flakes
1 (8-ounce) package shredded 4-Cheese Italian cheese
2 tablespoons grated Parmesan cheese
2 tablespoons dried Italian bread crumbs

Up to 1 month ahead or early in the day: Place 1 tablespoon salt in a large pot of water over high heat. When water comes to a boil, add ziti and cook, stirring occasionally, until pasta is al dente, about 10 to 12 minutes. Drain pasta in a colander.

Meanwhile, place tomatoes with juices, chicken, basil, oregano, mozzarella cheese, evaporated milk, garlic, 1 teaspoon salt, and red pepper flakes in a large bowl. Stir to combine ingredients well. Gently fold in cooked ziti.

Coat the bottom and sides of each of two 1½-quart baking dishes with vegetable cooking spray. Divide ziti mixture evenly between the two dishes. Spread half the shredded 4-Cheese Italian atop each casserole. Sprinkle 1 tablespoon Parmesan cheese and 1 tablespoon bread crumbs over each casserole. Cover each dish with plastic wrap and then aluminum foil. Refrigerate one and freeze the other until needed.

To bake: Preheat oven to 350°F. Remove foil and plastic wrap from baking dish. Re-cover dish with aluminum foil. Bake for 25 to 30 minutes, until heated through. Remove foil and bake for 5 minutes more, until top is browned. (If frozen, defrost casserole and bring to room temperature before baking.)

Hefty brand now offers 1½-quart foil casserole pans, which are perfect for this dish.

Serves: 8 to 12 (each casserole serves 4 to 6)

Chicken-Spinach Quiches

Double your pleasure with this recipe, which makes two deep-dish quiches. Serve one to your family for lunch or dinner today and freeze one for a later date.

2 (9-inch) frozen deep-dish pie crusts, thawed for 10 minutes

1 tablespoon butter

1 cup chopped sweet onions, like Vidalia

1 cup chopped red bell peppers

1 (9-ounce) bag baby spinach

8 eggs

1 cup ricotta cheese

½ teaspoon salt

½ teaspoon pepper

¼ teaspoon nutmeg

1 teaspoon dried basil

1 teaspoon Worcestershire sauce

1 teaspoon hot sauce

2 cups shredded sharp cheddar cheese, divided

3 cups diced, leftover Beer Can Chicken

¼ cup Parmesan cheese, divided

Up to 1 month ahead: Preheat oven to 375°F. Prick a few holes in bottom of pie crusts with a fork. Bake pie crusts for 5 minutes. Remove from oven and allow them to cool.

Place butter in a large nonstick skillet over medium heat. Add onions and bell peppers and sauté, stirring frequently, for 4 minutes, until vegetables are soft. Add spinach and sauté, stirring constantly, until spinach has wilted and mixture has cooked dry. Remove skillet from heat and allow vegetables to cool.

Meanwhile, place eggs, ricotta cheese, salt, pepper, nutmeg, basil, Worcestershire sauce, and hot sauce in a large bowl. Whisk to mix ingredients together well.

Place 1 cup cheddar cheese evenly in the bottom of each pie crust. Place half the spinach mixture evenly in each pie crust atop the cheeses. Place half the diced chicken (about 1½ cups) in each pie crust atop spinach mixture. Pour half the egg batter (about 1½ cups) into each pie crust.

Make a foil collar about 3 inches wide out of aluminum foil for each pie crust. Place collar around edges of crusts. Place quiches on a baking sheet in the oven. Bake for 30 minutes. (If you plan on serving one or both of the quiches immediately, increase baking time to 45 minutes and disregard the directions that follow.) Remove from oven and allow quiches to cool. Remove foil collars. Cover quiches with several sheets of aluminum foil. Refrigerate or freeze until needed.

To serve: Defrost quiche to room temperature. Preheat oven to 375°F. Sprinkle 2 tablespoons Parmesan cheese atop quiche. Place a foil collar around edge of crust. Place quiche on a baking sheet. Bake quiche for 30 minutes or until heated through.

You can substitute 1½ cups of other cooked vegetables, like leftover broccoli or asparagus, for the spinach in this recipe. And you can substitute other leftover protein, like beef, pork, or shrimp for the chicken.   **Serves:** 12 (each quiche serves 6)

Lemon-Mint Chicken Kabobs atop Rainbow Salsa

This is a great way to use chicken breasts of varying weights, which you often get when you buy in bulk. Weigh breasts and label each before freezing so you know how much poundage you have.

2 ears cooked corn-on-the-cob,
  kernels removed (about 2 cups)

1 large tomato, seeded, and diced
  (about 2 cups)

1 large orange, peeled, seeded and diced
  (about 1 cup)

¼ cup diced red bell peppers

¼ cup diced green bell peppers

½ cup finely chopped red onions

2 tablespoons orange marmalade

3 tablespoons cider vinegar

1 teaspoon salt, divided

¾ teaspoon freshly ground black pepper,
  divided

6 tablespoons fresh lemon juice
  (juice from 2 large lemons)

2 tablespoons olive oil

4 teaspoons garlic paste or
  finely minced garlic

¼ cup snipped fresh mint

3 pounds boneless, skinless chicken breasts,
  cut across grain into ½-inch slices

Up to 2 days ahead: Place corn, tomatoes, oranges, peppers, and onions in a large covered container. Mix marmalade, vinegar, ½ teaspoon salt, and ¼ teaspoon pepper together in a small bowl. Pour dressing over fruit and vegetable mixture and toss to combine ingredients well. Cover and refrigerate at least 2 hours so that flavors marry. (Makes 6 cups.)

At least 2 hours or up to 4 hours ahead: Place lemon juice, oil, garlic, mint, ½ teaspoon salt, and ½ teaspoon pepper in a medium bowl. Whisk to mix well. Add chicken slices and toss until chicken is well-coated with marinade mixture. Cover and refrigerate for at least 2 hours.

To grill: Remove chicken from marinade. Place marinade in a microwave-safe bowl and reheat for 1 minute. Thread chicken on 8 metal skewers. Preheat gas grill to medium-hot. Place skewers on grill and grill, turning frequently and basting with marinade, for 10 to 15 minutes or until chicken just loses its pink color and becomes opaque. (Do not overcook; chicken will continue cooking after it is removed from the grill.) Drain salsa in a colander, reserving juices. Place about ½ cup salsa on each dinner plate. Serve one skewer per person atop salsa. Serve remaining salsa in a bowl on the side.

Grate the orange rind before peeling the orange and grate the lemon rind before squeezing the lemons. Freeze grated rind in plastic wrap for future use.

Serves: 8 or 4 with leftovers

Rainbow Chicken Stir-Fry

Leftovers from Coconut Jasmine Sticky Rice and Lemon-Mint Chicken Kabobs atop Rainbow Salsa transform into a flavorful one-dish meal. Serve this stir-fry with a tossed green salad.

1½ cups diced leftover Lemon-Mint Chicken
1½ cups leftover Coconut Jasmine Sticky Rice (recipe page 84)
2 cups leftover Rainbow Salsa
3 tablespoons juice from Rainbow Salsa
3 tablespoons butter
½ cup chopped honey-roasted peanuts
½ teaspoon salt
¼ teaspoon freshly ground black pepper

One hour ahead: Toss together chicken, rice, salsa, and salsa juice in a large covered container. Refrigerate for 1 hour or up to 2 hours.

To cook: Melt butter in a large nonstick skillet over medium heat. Add peanuts and sauté, stirring occasionally, for 1 minute. Add rice mixture and stir to incorporate peanuts and butter. Reduce heat to medium-low and cook, stirring frequently, for 10 minutes, or until mixture is heated through.

Seasonings are based on the proportions of chicken, rice, and salsa listed above. Adjust seasonings as needed for the amount of leftovers you are using.

Serves: 4

Lime-Mustard Grilled Chicken Breasts

The key to moist grilled chicken is to not overcook it. Don't be afraid to cut into one of the grilled chicken breasts to check its internal temperature. Perfectly grilled chicken has just lost its pink, translucent color. The chicken will continue to cook once you remove it from the grill.

½ cup Dijon mustard

¼ cup brown sugar

2 tablespoons fresh lime juice

2 teaspoons garlic paste or finely minced garlic

½ teaspoon black pepper

¼ cup plus 2 tablespoons water

1 tablespoon olive oil

3 pounds boneless, skinless chicken breasts

At least 6 hours and up to 1 day ahead: Mix mustard, brown sugar, lime juice, garlic, pepper, and water together in a medium bowl. Whisk in olive oil. Place chicken breasts in a freezer-weight zipper bag. Pour marinade over chicken and close bag securely. Massage chicken in bag until well covered with marinade. Refrigerate until needed.

To grill: Preheat a gas grill to medium hot (about 450°F). Remove chicken breasts from marinade. Place marinade in a microwave-safe bowl and reheat for 1 minute. Grill chicken for 8 minutes. Turn chicken breasts and baste with marinade. Grill for 8 minutes more, until chicken is no longer pink when tested with a knife-cut in the center and has just lost its translucency. Remove from grill and cut into ½-inch slices. Serve immediately.

You can substitute raspberry wine vinegar for the lime juice for a different but equally flavorful dish.

Serves: 6 or 4 with leftovers

Cuban Chicken Salad in a Crispy Bread Bowl

Nothing says Cuba like mangos and black beans. And served in a showy toasted bread bowl, you can have your bread and eat it too! Simply tear off pieces of bread and eat them with your salad.

¾ cup mayonnaise

1½ teaspoons grated orange peel

2 teaspoons gingerroot paste or finely minced gingerroot

¼ cup mango chutney

¼ cup orange marmalade

2 cups frozen mango, cut into ½-inch dice, defrosted and drained

2 cups diced leftover Lime-Mustard Grilled Chicken Breasts

2 ounces pepper jack cheese, cut into slivers

1 (15.5-ounce) can black beans, rinsed and drained

¾ cup quartered grape tomatoes

1 cup diced celery

½ cup sliced scallions, white and green parts

Salt and freshly ground black pepper

4 petite round white fresh bread loaves

4 tablespoons butter

1 teaspoon garlic powder

4 cups shredded romaine lettuce hearts

½ cup sliced almonds, dry toasted

Up to 6 hours ahead: Mix mayonnaise, orange peel, gingerroot, chutney, and marmalade together in a medium bowl. Refrigerate until needed.

Toss together mango, chicken, cheese, black beans, tomatoes, celery, and scallions in a large bowl. Add dressing and toss to combine well. Add salt and pepper to taste. Transfer salad to a covered container and refrigerate until needed.

To bake: Preheat oven to 425°F. Cut the top off each round loaf of bread. Carefully pull out bread crumbs until only a shell remains. Melt butter in a microwave-safe bowl. Whisk in garlic powder. Brush insides and top edges of bread bowls with melted butter. Place directly on oven rack and bake for 10 minutes.

To serve: Transfer chicken salad to a large bowl. Toss with shredded lettuce and toasted almonds. Divide salad among the 4 bread bowls. Serve immediately.

Process the bits of bread you pull out of the bread bowls in a food processor to make fresh bread crumbs. Put them in a freezer-weight zipper bag and freeze for future use.

Serves: 4

Chicken Barbecue Pizza

Yam Good Sauce is a local North Carolina favorite available in specialty markets all over the state and by order on the Internet. Many regions of the country offer their own special prepared barbecue sauces. Try one in this easy recipe.

1 cup sliced and slivered leftover Lime-Mustard Grilled Chicken Breasts

½ cup Yam Good Sauce or other sweet and smoky barbecue sauce, divided

1 prepared pizza crust, such as Mama Mary's Thin Pizza Crust or Boboli

½ cup thinly sliced and slivered red onions

½ cup thinly sliced button or baby bella mushrooms

2 tablespoons slivered sun-dried tomatoes

1 tablespoon pine nuts

1 (8-ounce) package shredded Monterey Jack cheese

Preheat oven to 450°F. Mix chicken and ¼ cup barbecue sauce together in a small bowl. Place pizza crust on a pizza baking sheet or stone. Spread remaining ¼ cup sauce evenly over pizza. Place slivered chicken evenly over pizza. Sprinkle pizza with onions, mushrooms, sun-dried tomatoes, and pine nuts. Smother pizza toppings with shredded cheese.

Reduce oven heat to 425°F. Bake pizza for 8 minutes, until cheese has melted and is bubbly and ingredients have heated through. Serve immediately.

Check Web sites of Yam Good Sauce (www.alandmosfoods.com), Mama Mary's (www.mamamarys.com), or Boboli (www.boboli.com) to find where these products can be found near you or how you can order them. (Crusts are found in the main aisles of the supermarket, not in the freezer or refrigerated sections.) You can, of course, substitute your favorite sweet and smoky barbecue sauce, your preferred prepared pizza crust, and your vegetables of choice.

Serves: 4 (2 pieces each)

Grill-roasted Turkey with Orange-Molasses Glaze

Turkey is not just a holiday meal anymore! Once you grill-roast a turkey, you'll never roast one in your oven again. The turkey cooks in half the time recommended for oven roasting and needs your attention only for the final 15 minutes.

14- to 16-pound turkey
Olive oil spray or ¼ cup olive or canola oil
Poultry seasoning rub
1 cup orange juice
1 tablespoon molasses
1 tablespoon white wine vinegar
1 tablespoon dry mustard

Preheat gas grill for 15 minutes with all burners on low heat (400°F). Remove giblets and neck from turkey and discard. Rinse turkey and pat dry. Brush skin of turkey with olive oil or canola oil or coat with olive oil spray. Sprinkle your favorite poultry seasoning over entire surface of turkey and rub into skin.

Place turkey in an aluminum foil disposable roasting pan that has been coated with olive oil spray. Place a tent of aluminum foil over turkey and seal tightly. Place pan on the grill rack and close lid. Cook for 3 hours, or until popper is exposed or turkey leg can be pulled away from the body.

Meanwhile, make Orange-Molasses Glaze. Whisk orange juice, molasses, vinegar, and dry mustard together in a small saucepan over medium heat. Bring to a boil and cook for 2 minutes, until glaze reduces slightly. Remove from heat and transfer to a small bowl.

Remove tenting from turkey. Baste turkey with glaze. Close grill lid and cook 15 minutes more, basting every 5 minutes, until bird is golden brown. Remove turkey from grill and allow it to sit 5 minutes. Carve turkey, place on a large platter, and serve immediately.

🍴 Do not use a self-basting turkey. Do not open the grill lid to check on the turkey while it is roasting, because you'll cause the heat in the grill to drop significantly and it will take longer for the bird to cook. You can substitute pomegranate or cranberry juice for the orange juice if desired. Also, you can place your favorite stuffing in the turkey cavity just before grilling. Remove cooked stuffing before carving the turkey.

Serves: 8 to 10 with leftovers

Oven-roasted Lemon-Herb Turkey Breast

This turkey breast proves that turkey doesn't have to be served only on Thanksgiving. Easy to prepare, the juicy white meat lends itself to a potpourri of tasty leftover makeovers.

1 (8-pound) frozen turkey breast
Olive oil spray or olive oil
Lemon-herb or lemon-pepper seasoning

Place turkey in a sink full of cold water until defrosted. Refrigerate until needed.

Preheat oven to 350°F. Rinse and dry turkey. Coat turkey breast with olive oil spray or brush with olive oil. Sprinkle seasoning over entire turkey breast. Place turkey on a wire rack in a large baking pan. Bake for 2½ hours, until turkey breast, when tested with a knife, is just cooked through and no longer pink.

Remove from oven and allow turkey to rest at room temperature for 5 minutes. Serve immediately or cover with aluminum foil and refrigerate until needed.

Cut the white meat off the carcass before refrigerating in zipper bags. Freeze the carcass to make homemade turkey broth.

Serves: A crowd or a small group with lots of leftovers

Chardonnay-Alfredo Turkey Salad Stuffed Shells

These savory shells combine the crunch of turkey salad with creamy Alfredo cheesiness.

Salt

1 (12-ounce) box jumbo pasta shells

3 cups finely chopped leftover Grill-roasted Turkey or Oven-roasted Turkey Breast

⅓ cup chopped scallions

¾ cup chopped celery

⅓ cup finely chopped baby carrots

⅓ cup chopped red bell peppers

¼ cup sliced almonds, dry-toasted

2 cups chopped, peeled, and cored sweet-tart apples

⅔ cup mayonnaise

½ cup crumbled goat cheese

2 tablespoons lemon juice

Freshly ground black pepper

6 tablespoons butter

2 (1.25-ounce) packages McCormick Creamy Garlic Alfredo Sauce Mix

2 cups milk

2 tablespoons chardonnay wine

Parmesan cheese

Up to 1 day ahead: Add 1 teaspoon salt to a large pot of water. Place over high heat and bring to a boil. Add pasta shells, reduce heat to medium-high, and cook to al dente following manufacturer's instructions, about 10 minutes. Transfer shells with a slotted spoon to a colander and drain.

Place turkey, scallions, celery, carrots, bell peppers, almonds, and apples in a large bowl. Toss to combine. Mix mayonnaise, goat cheese, and lemon juice together in a small bowl. Add mayonnaise mixture to turkey mixture and toss until all ingredients are well coated with dressing. Season salad with salt and pepper to taste. Using a small spoon, stuff cooked pasta shells with turkey salad. Place stuffed shells in a covered container and refrigerate or freeze until needed.

To bake: Preheat oven to 350°F. Melt butter in a medium saucepan over medium heat. Add Alfredo sauce mix and milk. Whisk to combine. Bring to a boil, reduce heat to low, and simmer for 2 minutes, whisking frequently. Whisk in wine and remove from heat.

Coat a 10x13-inch baking dish with vegetable cooking spray. Spread 1 cup Alfredo sauce in bottom of dish. Place defrosted stuffed shells atop sauce in a tight-fitting single layer. Pour remaining Alfredo sauce over stuffed shells. Cover tightly with aluminum foil. Bake for 20 minutes. Remove foil and bake 10 minutes more. Sprinkle Parmesan cheese over each serving.

 Serve with a tossed salad and a freshly baked loaf of crunchy bread.

Serves: 6

Turkey and Ham Cannelloni

*Cannelloni is a great way to transform leftover turkey and ham into a tasty, elegant meal.
It differs from its stuffed cousin, manicotti, because it is smothered in a cheesy white
sauce instead of a tomato-based sauce.*

¾ teaspoon salt, divided

1 (8-ounce) package dried manicotti tubular shells

1 tablespoon olive oil

1 cup chopped onions

2 teaspoons garlic paste or finely minced garlic

1 (9-ounce) bag baby spinach

1½ cups finely diced leftover Grill-roasted Turkey or Oven-roasted Turkey Breast

1½ cups finely diced Orange-Mustard Glazed Ham (recipe page 33) or other ham

2 large eggs, beaten

2½ cups part-skim ricotta cheese

1 tablespoon snipped fresh chives

2 tablespoons snipped fresh flat-leaf parsley

1 teaspoon snipped fresh thyme

1 tablespoon grated lemon peel (rind of 1 lemon)

¼ teaspoon black pepper

4 tablespoons (½ stick) butter

2 (1.5-ounce) packages McCormick Four Cheese Sauce Mix

2½ cups milk

⅓ cup Parmesan cheese

Up to 3 months ahead: Add ½ teaspoon salt to a large pot of water. Place pot over high
heat and bring to a boil. Add pasta and cook to al dente following manufacturer's instructions,
about 10 minutes. Carefully transfer pasta with a slotted spoon to a colander. Transfer
drained pasta tubes to a nonstick baking sheet and set aside.

Meanwhile, place oil in a large nonstick skillet over medium heat. Add onions and garlic
and sauté, stirring frequently, until onions are soft, about 2 minutes. Add spinach and sauté,
stirring constantly, until spinach has wilted and its released water has evaporated, about 2
minutes. Transfer spinach to a colander. Press on spinach with the back of a spoon to drain
off remaining liquid.

Place spinach mixture, turkey, ham, eggs, ricotta cheese, chives, parsley, thyme, grated lemon peel, ¼ teaspoon salt, and pepper in a large bowl. Toss with a large spoon until ingredients are well combined.

Melt butter in a medium saucepan over medium heat. Add cheese sauce mix and milk. Whisk to combine. Bring to a boil, whisking constantly. Reduce heat to low and cook for 2 minutes, whisking frequently.

To assemble cannelloni: Coat a 10x13-inch baking dish with vegetable cooking spray. Spread 1 cup cheese sauce in the bottom of baking dish. Working with one pasta tube at a time, using a small spoon, stuff filling into tube and place in baking dish. Continue with all tubes or until dish is filled with a tightly packed single layer of filled cannelloni. Pour remaining cheese sauce over stuffed cannelloni. Sprinkle with Parmesan cheese. Cover with plastic wrap and aluminum foil and refrigerate or freeze until needed.

To bake: Preheat oven to 350°F. Bring cannelloni to room temperature. Remove foil and plastic wrap. Cover again with foil. Bake for 30 to 40 minutes. (Cannelloni will be done when it is browned and bubbly around the edges.)

You can substitute dried herbs for the fresh, if necessary. When using dried herbs, use one-third the amount specified for fresh herbs.

Serves: 6

Roast Duck with Fruited Orange Sauce

Ducks are fatty birds. Baking them usually means a lot of splattering grease in the bottom of the pan, which makes many cooks think the process is just too much trouble. Roasting a duck is actually very easy and not messy at all when you stuff the cavities with oranges. The juice from the oranges drips into the pan and keeps the grease from burning.

1 cup orange juice

1 cup orange marmalade

1 tablespoon cornstarch

2 tablespoons fresh lemon juice

2 cups frozen peach slices, cut in ¼-inch dice

2 bananas, sliced in half lengthwise and cut into ¼-inch pieces

1 tablespoon orange liqueur

1 tablespoon grated orange peel

2 whole defrosted ducks, giblets removed

2 large navel oranges

McCormick Garlic and Herb seasoning

Early in the day: Place orange juice and marmalade in a medium nonstick saucepan over medium heat. Stir until marmalade has dissolved, about 1 minute. Whisk cornstarch and lemon juice together in a small bowl. Add to orange juice mixture. Whisk until thickened slightly, about 2 minutes. Stir in peaches, bananas, orange liqueur, and orange peel. Remove from heat. Transfer to a covered container and refrigerate until needed. (Makes 4 cups.)

About 3 hours ahead: Preheat oven to 425°F. Rinse ducks, inside and out, and dry with paper toweling. Cut away excess fat with kitchen scissors, including neck flaps and tails. Cut each orange into eight pieces. Stuff each duck cavity with oranges. Sprinkle all surfaces of each duck liberally with garlic and herb seasoning. Rub seasoning into skin. Transfer ducks to a wire rack placed in a large aluminum roasting pan.

Bake ducks for 30 minutes at 425°F. Reduce heat to 350°F and bake for 1½ hours more. Increase heat to 425°F and bake for another 20 minutes, until skin is crispy and juices near leg joint run clear when tested with a knife.

To finish: About 15 minutes before serving, place orange sauce in a medium nonstick saucepan over low heat until heated through.

Remove oranges from duck cavities and discard. Cut each duck in half through the breastbone and on either side of the backbone. Discard the backbones. Cut each piece in half again, creating 4 breast/wing quarters and 4 leg/thigh quarters.

Serve duck with fruited orange sauce.

You'll need an extra orange for the grated orange peel if you don't already have some on hand in your freezer pantry. After grating the peel, squeeze the orange and use the juice in the sauce.

To store leftover duck, remove skin and store in a small zipper bag. Remove meat from bones and store in a separate zipper bag. Discard carcass.

Serves: 8 or 6 with leftovers

Faux Peking Duck

In this knockoff of the classic Peking duck found in most every Chinese restaurant in the world, sautéed flour tortillas are substituted for the difficult-to-find de rigueur Mandarin pancakes.

¼ cup hoisin sauce

⅓ cup plum sauce

1½ cups thinly sliced leftover Roast Duck breast meat

¼ cup thinly sliced leftover Roast Duck crispy skin

6 (6.5-inch) flour tortillas

10 scallions, white parts only, quartered lengthwise and shredded

1½ cups julienne-cut peeled English cucumbers

Preheat oven to 250°F. Whisk hoisin and plum sauces together in a small bowl. Place duck breast on a microwavable plate and reheat for 1 minute. Place duck skin in a small nonstick skillet over medium heat. Cook for 1 minute, stirring frequently, until skin crisps up.

Place a small nonstick skillet coated with olive oil spray over medium heat. Working with 1 tortilla at a time, place tortilla in skillet. Cook 30 seconds. Turn tortilla over with tongs. Spread sauce mixture liberally over tortilla with a basting brush. Spread about ¼ cup duck breast on half the tortilla. Top with a sprinkling of scallions and about ¼ cup cucumbers. Drizzle a little sauce over duck mixture. Using tongs, fold bottom half of tortilla over filling. Press on tortilla for a few seconds. Transfer folded tortilla with tongs to a nonstick baking sheet and place in the oven. Repeat process with the remaining 5 tortillas. Serve with extra sauce.

Two breast quarters should yield the amount of duck recommended in this recipe.

Serves: 3 (2 tortillas per serving)

Duck-Noodle Salad in Crusty Baskets

This light, elegant salad is the perfect dish to serve at a buffet luncheon because it comes in its own edible bowl.

Vegetable cooking spray

4 egg roll wrappers (6-inch-square)

1 tablespoon Asian sweet chili sauce

2 teaspoons fish sauce

6 tablespoons fresh lime juice

1 tablespoon honey

1 teaspoon salt

1½ ounces dry rice noodles, broken in half

1 heaping cup peeled, julienne-cut
    English cucumbers

½ cup roughly chopped red onions

½ cup celery, sliced thin on the diagonal

2 cups sliced leftover Roast Duck leg
    and thigh meat

¼ cup snipped fresh flat-leaf parsley

2 tablespoons snipped fresh mint leaves

6 tablespoons chopped fruit-and-nut
    trail mix

Preheat oven to 350°F. Place 4 round ovenproof ramekins (¾-cup) upside down on a non-stick baking sheet. Coat ramekins with vegetable cooking spray. Drape 1 egg roll wrapper over each ramekin, pressing wrapper against ramekin to form a basket shape. Coat surface of egg roll wrappers with vegetable cooking spray. Bake for 13 to 15 minutes, until golden brown and crusty. Remove from oven and allow baskets to cool. Gently remove ramekins from shells. Place shells on a wire rack until needed.

Meanwhile, whisk chili sauce, fish sauce, lime juice, and honey together in a small bowl. Cover and refrigerate until needed.

Fill a medium saucepan with water and add salt. Bring to boil over medium heat. Add rice noodles and cook until al dente, 2 to 3 minutes. Drain in a colander. Rinse with cold water and drain thoroughly.

Place cucumbers, onions, celery, duck, parsley, mint, and noodles in a large mixing bowl. Pour dressing over mixture and toss until all ingredients are well coated. Divide duck salad among the 4 crusty baskets. Sprinkle 1½ tablespoons chopped trail mix atop salad. Serve immediately.

You can make the crusty baskets early in the day and store in an airtight container until needed. You can substitute chicken thigh meat for the duck for an equally tasty salad. Be sure to cut either bird into bite-size pieces.

Serves: 4

Roasted Orange-Sesame Pork Loin

If you have the time, marinate this pork loin for the full two days. The longer it marinates, the better it tastes.

2 tablespoons soy sauce

1 tablespoon raspberry vinegar

½ cup fresh orange juice

1 teaspoon gingerroot paste or minced gingerroot

1½ teaspoons garlic paste or minced garlic

1 scallion, chopped

¼ cup honey

¼ teaspoon crushed red pepper flakes

¼ teaspoon lemon sea salt or ¼ teaspoon salt and ½ teaspoon fresh lemon juice

2 tablespoons coconut rum (optional) or 2 teaspoons coconut extract

2 tablespoons sesame oil

¼ cup plus 2 tablespoons canola oil

1 (3½-pound) boneless pork loin roast

Up to 2 days ahead: Place soy sauce, vinegar, orange juice, gingerroot, garlic, scallions, honey, crushed red pepper flakes, lemon sea salt, and rum in a blender, and pulse until smooth. With motor running at lowest speed, slowly pour in sesame and canola oils.

Place pork roast in a large freezer-weight zipper bag. Pour marinade over roast. Close bag and massage roast until it is totally covered with marinade. Refrigerate at least 24 hours or up to 2 days to tenderize pork.

To roast: Preheat oven to 425°F. Remove pork from bag, discarding marinade. Set a grill rack, coated with vegetable cooking spray, in a large baking pan. Fill pan with 1 inch water. Place pork on rack and place pan in oven.

Roast pork for 15 minutes. Reduce heat to 375°F. Roast pork for 30 to 40 more minutes, until it is still slightly pink in the middle.

Remove roast from oven, cover it with aluminum foil, and allow it to rest for 10 minutes. (Pork will continue to cook.) Cut pork into thin (⅛-inch) slices against the grain.

Even a small sprinkling of lemon sea salt imparts a wonderful lemony flavor to food. You can order it online from Bellamessa: www.opal-export.com.

Serves: 12 or 6 with leftovers

Pork Pad Thai

This is one of my all-time favorite dishes. Every time I find fresh bean sprouts at the supermarket I make this recipe.

1 pound Roasted Orange-Sesame
    Pork Loin slices

6 tablespoons fish sauce

½ cup ketchup

¼ cup sugar

6 tablespoons water

⅔ cup chopped peanuts

½ cup chopped scallions

½ cup chopped fresh flat-leaf parsley

1 teaspoon crushed red pepper flakes

2 (9-ounce) packages fresh fettuccine
    noodles

2 tablespoons olive oil

1 tablespoon canola oil

3 tablespoons plus 1 teaspoon garlic paste
    or finely minced garlic

4 large eggs, lightly beaten

4 cups bean sprouts, washed and dried

2 limes, cut into 12 wedges

Early in the day: Cut pork slices in half lengthwise, then cut into ¼-inch slivers crosswise. Cover and refrigerate until needed.

Combine fish sauce, ketchup, sugar, and 6 tablespoons water in a small bowl. Stir to combine. Place in a covered container and refrigerate until needed.

Place peanuts, scallions, parsley, and red pepper flakes in a small bowl. Stir to combine. Place in a covered container and refrigerate until needed.

Fifteen minutes before serving: Bring a large pot of water to boil over high heat. Add fettuccine noodles, reduce heat to medium-high, and cook to al dente following package directions, about 3 minutes. Drain pasta in a colander and toss with olive oil. Set aside.

Place 1 tablespoon canola oil in a large nonstick wok or skillet over medium-high heat. Add garlic. Stir-fry for 30 seconds. Add eggs and stir-fry for 30 seconds. Add cooked fettuccine noodles, ketchup mixture, and pork, and stir-fry for 2 minutes, tossing ingredients constantly to coat well with sauce. Add bean sprouts and stir-fry for 15 seconds. Remove from heat and transfer to a large serving bowl. Sprinkle with peanut mixture and serve with lime wedges.

You can cut up the Roasted Orange Sesame Pork Loin slices and freeze in 1 pound packages for up to 1 month. Defrost before proceeding with this recipe. You can use any leftover meat or seafood in this dish. Substitute wide rice noodles for the fettuccine, if you want a more authentically Thai version of this dish.

Serves: 6

Mu Shu Lettuce Wraps

Traditionally Mu Shu Pork is served in Mandarin pancakes. Wrapped in lettuce leaves, these Chinese knockoffs eliminate the carbohydrates and ramp up the Asian flavors.

1½ cups diced leftover Roasted Orange-Sesame Pork Loin

3 tablespoons plum sauce

7½ tablespoons soy sauce, divided

4½ tablespoons white wine

1½ tablespoons sugar

1½ tablespoons sesame oil

1 tablespoon cornstarch

2 teaspoons canola oil

1½ cups shredded carrots

¾ cup thinly sliced yellow bell peppers

¾ cup thinly sliced red bell peppers

1½ cups sliced scallions

16 iceberg, Boston, bibb, or hydroponic lettuce leaves, rinsed and dried

2 tablespoons sesame seeds, dry-toasted

Up to 1 day ahead: Mix pork, plum sauce, and 1½ tablespoons soy sauce together in a medium bowl. Cover and refrigerate until needed.

Whisk 6 tablespoons soy sauce, wine, sugar, and sesame oil together in a medium bowl. Place cornstarch in a small bowl. Add 1 tablespoon soy-wine mixture and whisk until smooth. Whisk cornstarch into soy-wine mixture. Cover and refrigerate until needed.

Place canola oil in a large nonstick skillet over medium heat. Add pork and stir-fry for 1 minute. Add carrots, bell peppers, and scallions. Stir-fry 2 minutes. Add soy-wine mixture and stir fry for 2 minutes, until sauce has thickened. Cool for 1 minute.

To serve: Allow diners to make their own lettuce packets: Place a heaping kitchen tablespoonful of the pork mixture in the center of each lettuce leaf. Sprinkle with sesame seeds. Fold like an envelope and eat like a sandwich.

Served with a side of rice, the lettuce wraps make a light but satisfying dinner. For a stunning appetizer, put the filling in endive leaves and fan out the leaves on a serving platter.

Serves: 4

Orange-Mustard Glazed Baked Ham with Horseradish Cream Sauce

Your dinner guests may choose to enhance their ham with the orange-mustard glaze or the horseradish cream sauce, but the tastiest way to eat this ham is to drizzle the glaze over your serving of ham, then dip each bite in a side portion of the horseradish sauce.

1 (8- to 9-pound) spiral ham

½ cup Triple Sec liqueur

2 tablespoons cranberry honey mustard

½ cup orange juice

1 tablespoon grated orange peel

⅛ teaspoon plus a pinch ground nutmeg

¼ cup honey

1 teaspoon cracked black pepper

1 teaspoon coarse salt

½ cup heavy whipping cream

1 heaping tablespoon prepared horseradish

1 teaspoon white balsamic vinegar

Salt and freshly ground black pepper

Preheat oven to 350°F. Coat a shallow baking pan with vegetable cooking spray. Place ham, cut-side down, in pan. Cover with aluminum foil. Bake for 45 minutes.

Meanwhile, place liqueur, mustard, orange juice, orange peel, ⅛ teaspoon nutmeg, honey, cracked pepper, and coarse salt in a small saucepan over medium heat. Bring to a boil, stirring frequently. Reduce heat to low and simmer, stirring occasionally, for 5 minutes.

Place whipping cream in the bowl of an electric mixer. Beat cream until thick but not stiff, about 2 minutes. With mixer on low speed, fold in horseradish, vinegar, and salt and pepper to taste. Transfer to a small serving bowl and refrigerate until needed.

Remove foil from ham. Pour one-third of the orange-mustard glaze over ham. Bake for 10 minutes. Pour another one-third of glaze over ham. Bake for 10 minutes. Pour final third of glaze over ham and bake for 10 minutes more.

Remove ham from pan, cut spiral pieces away from the bone, and place on a serving platter. Pour orange-mustard glaze from bottom of pan into a small serving bowl. Serve orange-mustard glaze and horseradish cream sauce as enhancements with the ham.

Substitute your favorite orange liqueur for the Triple Sec; your favorite fruit honey mustard for the cranberry honey mustard; and white wine vinegar, chardonnay vinegar, or rice wine vinegar for the white balsamic vinegar.

Serves: 12 to 16 or 6 to 8 with leftovers.

Ham and Split Pea Soup

Because the ham and vegetables are pureed together in this soup, it is a mustard-olive color instead of the traditional "pea green." Pea soup lovers swear the flavor is out of this world.

1 pound green split peas

2 teaspoons olive oil

1 cup chopped sweet onions, like Vidalia

2 cups finely chopped carrots

1 cup roughly chopped celery

1 large potato, peeled and diced

2½ cups diced (½-inch) leftover Orange-Mustard Glazed Baked Ham

11 cups water

2 bay leaves

½ teaspoon dried thyme

2 teaspoons salt

½ teaspoon black pepper

The night before: Place split peas in a large pot with water to cover and soak overnight.

To cook: Place olive oil in a large nonstick soup pot over medium heat. Add onions, carrots, and celery and sauté, stirring occasionally, until onions are soft, about 3 minutes. Add potatoes, ham, water, bay leaves, and thyme. Stir to combine. Drain the split peas in a colander and add to the pot. Bring to a boil, reduce heat to low, cover, and cook, stirring occasionally for 1 hour.

Remove bay leaves and puree soup in a blender in batches until smooth. Transfer each pureed batch to a large bowl. Stir in salt and pepper, adding more to taste if desired. Wash and dry soup pot. Return soup to pot and reheat on low until heated through. Serve immediately or transfer to covered containers and refrigerate or freeze until needed.

If you prefer bits of ham in your pea soup, reserve ¾ cup of the ham, diced very finely, and add to the pureed soup.

Serves: 12 cups

Mini Ham Popovers

A great way to use leftover ham, these miniature popovers are great for breakfast, brunch, or as a side offering with a dinner salad. They can be made ahead and refrigerated or frozen, perfect for a spur-of-the-moment dinner decision.

1¼ cups finely diced Orange-Mustard Glazed Baked Ham
1¼ cups shredded sharp cheddar cheese
½ cup plus 2 tablespoons finely chopped red onions
6 eggs
2 cups half-and-half
½ cup butter, melted
6 hearty shakes hot pepper sauce
1 cup Bisquick
¼ cup grated Parmesan cheese
1 teaspoon dry mustard
1 tablespoon margarine or Crisco

Preheat oven to 375°F. Mix ham, cheddar cheese, and red onions together in a small bowl. Set aside.

Whisk eggs, half-and-half, butter, and hot pepper sauce together in a large bowl. Whisk in Bisquick, Parmesan cheese, and dry mustard.

Grease the cups of a mini muffin pan with margarine or Crisco. Place ½ tablespoon ham mixture in the bottom of each cup. Place egg mixture in a large measuring cup. Pour mixture into each mini muffin cup, filling to within ⅛ inch of the top. (Repeat process with each batch.)

Bake for 20 to 25 minutes, until golden brown and puffy. Remove popovers from oven and cool in pan for 5 minutes. Gently remove popovers with the tip of a thin knife. Serve immediately or cool on a wire rack and refrigerate or freeze until needed. Defrost popovers before reheating. Reheat refrigerated popovers on a nonstick baking sheet at 325°F for 5 minutes.

To freeze popovers, place in layers in a covered container. Place a sheet of waxed or parchment paper between layers. Popovers will defrost at room temperature in 5 minutes.

Makes: 54 mini popovers (serve 3 to 4 per person)

Spinach and Ham Calzones

Not quite the same as you'd find at your local pizzeria, but close enough. Hearty, comforting, and oozing with cheese, these calzones welcome an array of leftover ingredients. Substitute ingredients in proportions listed below.

1 tablespoon olive oil

1 cup chopped onions, like Vidalia

1 cup chopped red bell peppers

½ teaspoon Durkee's Citrus Grill seasoning or lemon pepper seasoning

1 (6-ounce) bag baby spinach, roughly chopped

1 (32-ounce) package Real New York Pizza Dough, defrosted at room temperature

1 tablespoon flour

2 cups diced leftover Orange-Mustard Glazed Baked Ham

½ cup ricotta cheese

4 cups shredded mozzarella cheese

1 egg, beaten

2 cups tomato and basil marinara sauce

Early in the day or up to 2 weeks ahead: Place oil in a large nonstick skillet over medium heat. Add onions, bell peppers, and citrus grill seasoning, and sauté, stirring frequently, until onions are soft, about 2 minutes. Add spinach and cook, stirring constantly, until spinach has wilted and its released liquid has evaporated, about 2 minutes more. Remove from heat and set aside.

Preheat oven to 375°F. Line a baking sheet with parchment paper. Cut each dough ball into 4 pieces. Spread flour on work surface. Work with one piece at a time and keep the rest covered with a damp cloth. With clean hands, shape each piece into a flattened circle. Grasp top edge of dough circle and stretch and rotate dough, enlarging the circle to 7 to 8 inches in diameter.

Place dough circle on the floured counter. On the lower half of the circle, place ¼ cup ham, 1 ¼ tablespoons spinach mixture, 1 tablespoon ricotta cheese, and ½ cup mozzarella cheese, leaving a ¾-inch border. Grasp opposite edge of dough and stretch it over filling, lining up edges. Press edges to seal and crimp the sealed dough with your fingers. Brush a very light coating of beaten egg over dough and transfer calzone to a parchment-paper-lined baking sheet. Repeat process with remaining dough balls.

Bake calzones for 20 minutes. (This will only partially bake them.) Remove calzones from oven and cool on a wire rack. When totally cool, transfer to a zipper bag and refrigerate or freeze until needed.

To serve: Preheat oven to 375°F. Defrost calzones to room temperature. Place on a nonstick baking sheet. Bake for 15 to 17 minutes, until golden. Place marinara sauce in a small saucepan over low heat until warmed through. Serve each calzone immediately with ¼ cup marinara sauce on the side for dipping.

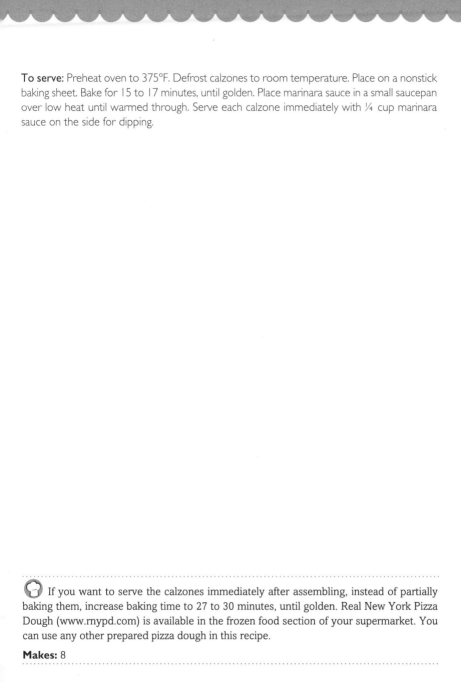 If you want to serve the calzones immediately after assembling, instead of partially baking them, increase baking time to 27 to 30 minutes, until golden. Real New York Pizza Dough (www.rnypd.com) is available in the frozen food section of your supermarket. You can use any other prepared pizza dough in this recipe.

Makes: 8

Grilled Peachy Pork Tenderloin

The grilled tenderloin is especially good when fresh peaches are in season, but frozen peach slices also work well in this recipe.

5 fresh freestone peaches

3 tablespoons honey

1 tablespoon cornstarch

1 tablespoon lemon juice

¼ cup water

½ teaspoon almond extract

1 teaspoon gingerroot paste or
    minced gingerroot

1 teaspoon garlic paste or minced garlic

1 teaspoon sesame oil

⅓ cup chopped scallions

⅛ teaspoon white pepper

2½ pounds pork tenderloin (2 tenderloins)

Up to 1 month ahead: Bring a medium saucepan of water to boil over high heat. Remove pan from heat and place on a hot pad. Place each peach in hot water for about 30 seconds. Remove peaches from water and peel and pit each one. Slice and dice peaches and place in a food processor. Add honey, cornstarch, lemon, water, and almond extract, and pulse to combine.

Place peach mixture in a medium saucepan over medium-low heat and cook for 10 minutes, until thick and bubbly. Remove pan from burner and allow mixture to cool. Transfer to three 1-cup covered containers. Refrigerate for up to 3 days or freeze until needed.

At least 24 hours or up to 2 days ahead: Mix together 1 cup peach marinade, gingerroot, garlic, sesame oil, scallions, and white pepper in a medium bowl.

Place pork in a zipper bag. Pour marinade over pork. Close zipper bag and massage bag so that pork is well coated with marinade. Refrigerate for at least 24 hours or up to 2 days, until needed.

To grill: Preheat gas grill to 450°F. Remove pork from marinade. Transfer marinade to a microwave-proof container. Microwave marinade for 1 minute. Place tenderloin on grill. Baste with marinade. Grill for a total of 15 minutes, turning and basting twice with marinade. Remove tenderloin from grill. Allow to rest for 5 minutes. (Pork will be pink, but will keep cooking while it is resting.) Slice tenderloin into ¾-inch medallions and serve immediately.

Use leftover pork tenderloin to make Pork Tenderloin Medallion Salad with Peach Vinaigrette Drizzle (recipe follows) and to make Pork Tenderloin-Orzo Soup (recipe page 81).

Serves: 10 or 4 with leftovers

Pork Tenderloin Medallion Salad with Peach Vinaigrette Drizzle

This recipe is best in the summer, when a plethora of peaches graces every fruit stand and farmer's market, but it also is a ray of sunshine in the winter if you use frozen peaches.

2 fresh freestone peaches

3 tablespoons red wine vinegar

2 tablespoons sugar

¼ teaspoon salt

¼ teaspoon dry mustard

3 tablespoons extra-virgin olive oil

6 cups mixed greens

3 chopped scallions

¼ cup seeded, diced tomato

¼ cup sliced almonds, toasted

2 tablespoons crumbled blue cheese

¼ cup broccoli slaw

16 slices Grilled Peachy Pork Tenderloin

For Peach Vinaigrette: Bring a medium saucepan of water to boil over high heat. Remove pan from heat and place on a hot pad. Place each peach in hot water for about 30 seconds. Remove peaches from water and peel and pit each one. Slice and dice peaches and place in a blender with vinegar, sugar, salt, and dry mustard. Puree until smooth. With blender at low speed, slowly add olive oil. Transfer to a covered container and refrigerate until needed. Bring to room temperature before serving. (Makes about 1 cup; keeps in refrigerator 1 week.)

For salad: Toss greens, scallions, tomatoes, almonds, blue cheese, and broccoli slaw with just enough vinaigrette to coat ingredients. (Don't use too much dressing or greens will get soggy.) Divide salad among 4 dinner plates.

Arrange 4 medallions pork tenderloin aside salad on each plate. Drizzle medallions with Peach Vinaigrette.

Serve with a side of corn-on-the-cob or freshly baked refrigerator rolls.

Serves: 4

Chinese Roast Pork Chops

Boneless pork loin tends to dry out during roasting. Frequently basting the boneless pork chops not only infuses them with Chinese flavors but ensures that they stay moist.

¼ cup hoisin sauce

2 tablespoons soy sauce

½ cup ketchup

2 tablespoons honey

2 tablespoons dry sherry

1 teaspoon gingerroot paste or finely minced gingerroot

2 teaspoons garlic paste or finely minced garlic

1¾ pounds boneless pork loin chops, cut 1-inch thick

One day ahead: Whisk together hoisin sauce, soy sauce, ketchup, honey, sherry, gingerroot, and garlic in a medium bowl. Place pork chops in a large freezer-weight zipper bag. Pour marinade over pork chops. Massage pork chops in bag so that all surfaces are coated with marinade. Close zipper bag and refrigerate overnight.

To bake: Preheat oven to 350°F. Place a sheet of aluminum foil in the bottom of a broiler pan. Coat broiler pan rack with vegetable cooking spray. Remove pork chops from marinade. Place pork chops on rack. Place marinade in a microwave-safe bowl. Reheat for 1 minute. Brush pork chops with marinade.

Bake pork chops for 15 minutes. Turn chops and brush with marinade. Bake for 15 minutes more. Turn chops again and brush with marinade. Bake chops for 10 minutes. Turn chops one more time and brush with marinade. Bake chops for a final 10 minutes.

Remove chops from oven and cut them into paper-thin slices on the diagonal. Reheat marinade in microwave for 1 minute. Serve pork with marinade sauce on the side.

Using thick boneless pork loin chops instead of a boneless loin roast allows you to more easily cut the slices paper-thin.

Serves: 6 or 4 with leftovers

Pork Fried Rice

No need to order takeout Chinese food when you stir-fry this authentic-tasting fried rice. Both rice and the Chinese Roast Pork Chops freeze wonderfully, so you can create this ethnic dish in minutes, any time you get a hankering for a taste of the Far East.

1 tablespoon plus 1 teaspoon canola oil, divided

2 eggs, beaten

1 tablespoon gingerroot paste or finely minced gingerroot

½ tablespoon garlic paste or finely minced garlic

2½ teaspoons Asian sweet chili sauce, divided

¼ cup fresh lime juice

3 tablespoons sherry

3 tablespoons oyster sauce

1½ tablespoons brown sugar

¾ cup thinly sliced sweet onions, like Vidalia

1 cup thinly sliced baby bella or button mushrooms

½ cup thinly sliced red bell peppers

9 ounces leftover slices Chinese Roast Pork Chops, cut into thin slivers (2 cups)

3 cups leftover Coconut Jasmine Sticky Rice (recipe page 84) or other cooked white rice

¼ cup chopped cashews

2 tablespoons snipped flat-leaf parsley

1 lime, cut into 8 pieces

Place 1 teaspoon canola oil in a large nonstick wok over medium heat. Add eggs and quickly swirl them around wok to form a very thin layer of egg (called an egg sheet). When egg sheet has set (about 30 seconds), loosen it with a rubber spatula and slide it onto a cutting board. With a sharp knife, slice egg sheet into ½-inch strips, then cut strips into 1½-inch lengths. Set aside. Wipe out wok with paper toweling.

Mix gingerroot, garlic, and 1 teaspoon chili sauce in a small bowl. Set aside. Whisk lime juice, sherry, oyster sauce, brown sugar, and 1½ teaspoons chili sauce mixture together in a medium bowl. Set aside.

Place 1 tablespoon oil in wok over medium heat. Add onions and gingerroot mixture and sauté, stirring constantly, for 1½ minutes. Add mushrooms and bell peppers and sauté, stirring constantly, for 1½ minutes. Add pork and lime juice mixture. Stir to mix well. Cook for 2 minutes, stirring occasionally. Stir in rice and cashews. Reduce heat to low and cook for 2 minutes, stirring occasionally. Stir in egg strips and parsley. Serve immediately. Garnish each serving with 2 lime wedges.

Cut peeled onion in half before thinly slicing it. Then cut the slices in half once again. Thinly slice the red bell pepper, then cut the slices into thirds.

Serves: 4

Pork Stir-Fry L'Orange over Crispy Noodle Cake

This one-dish meal is elegant enough to serve to company. Prepare sauces, cook pasta, and prep vegetables early in the day, and this healthy stir-fry comes together in minutes.

8 ounces dry capellini or angel hair pasta

½ cup leftover Ponzu Sauce (recipe page 61)

4 tablespoons canola oil, divided

1 tablespoon cornstarch

2 tablespoons soy sauce, divided

½ cup chicken broth

1½ tablespoons orange juice concentrate

1 tablespoon orange liqueur, like Cointreau or Grand Marnier

1 teaspoon grated orange peel

½ teaspoon toasted sesame oil

1 tablespoon gingerroot paste or finely minced gingerroot

½ tablespoon garlic paste or finely minced garlic

2 teaspoons Asian sweet chili sauce

3 scallions, thinly sliced

1 cup baby carrots, quartered lengthwise

1 cup snow pea pods, cut in half crosswise

1 cup thinly sliced red bell peppers, cut in half crosswise

1 cup thinly sliced baby bella or button mushrooms

1 cup julienne-cut zucchini

9 ounces leftover sliced Chinese Roast Pork Chops, cut into ¾-inch pieces

4 ounces bean sprouts

Bring a large pot of water to boil over high heat. Add capellini and cook to al dente, following manufacturer's instructions, about 4 minutes. Drain in a colander. Return capellini to pot and toss with Ponzu Sauce.

Preheat oven to 300°F. Place a 12-inch nonstick skillet over medium heat. Add 2 tablespoons oil. Spread capellini in skillet in an even layer. Cook for 4 minutes, until underside of noodles are light brown and crispy. Invert skillet on a large platter. Using a firm spatula, slide noodle cake back into skillet. Cook 2 minutes more, until underside of noodle cake is golden and crispy. Invert on an ovenproof platter and place noodle cake in oven to keep warm while you make the stir-fry.

Whisk together cornstarch and 1 tablespoon soy sauce in a medium bowl. When smooth, whisk in remaining 1 tablespoon soy sauce, chicken broth, orange juice concentrate, orange liqueur, orange peel, and sesame oil. Set aside until needed.

Place a nonstick wok over medium heat. Add remaining 2 tablespoons canola oil. When oil is hot, add gingerroot, garlic, chili sauce, and scallions. Stir-fry for 30 seconds. Add carrots and stir-fry 1 minute. Stirring constantly, add snow peas and bell peppers and stir-fry 1 minute; add mushrooms and zucchini and stir-fry 1 minute; then pork and orange sauce and stir-fry 1 minute, until sauce thickens. Remove stir-fry from heat, add bean sprouts, and toss to combine.

Remove noodle cake from oven. Cut into 6 wedges. Top each wedge with a portion of the stir-fry. Place one stir-fry-topped noodle cake wedge on each dinner plate and serve immediately.

You can use leftover peanut sauce from the Caribbean Shrimp Wraps (recipe page 72) instead of the Ponzu Sauce to create a peanut noodle cake. Use leftover angel hair or spaghetti if you have it. Substitute any of your favorite fresh vegetables in the same proportions as those listed in this recipe. If you don't have orange juice concentrate on hand, you can substitute orange juice, but the orange flavor will not be as prevalent.

Serves: 6

Aunt Rita's Tried-and-True Two-Bean Chili

I recently found this recipe on a yellowed, well-splattered card in my mother's recipe file. Her younger sister's chili lives up to its tried-and-true boast. It is the best I've ever tasted.

1 teaspoon olive oil

1 cup chopped sweet onions, like Vidalia

1 pound ground beef (90 percent lean)

3 teaspoons garlic paste or finely minced garlic

½ cup chopped green bell pepper

1 (14.5-ounce) can stewed tomatoes with onions, celery, and green peppers, with juices

1 (14.5-ounce) can stewed tomatoes with basil, garlic, and oregano, with juices

2 teaspoons instant bouillon dissolved in 2 cups boiling water (or 2 cups beef broth)

1 (8-ounce) can tomato sauce

1 tablespoon chili powder

1 teaspoon salt

1 teaspoon ground cumin

⅛ teaspoon cayenne pepper

1 (15-ounce) can black beans, rinsed and drained

1 (15.8-ounce) can great northern beans, rinsed and drained

Place olive oil in a large soup pot over medium heat. Add onions, ground beef, and garlic. Cook, stirring frequently, until onions are soft and beef is almost cooked through, about 3½ minutes. Add bell peppers and cook, stirring frequently, for 1½ minutes more. Add stewed tomatoes, beef broth, tomato sauce, chili powder, salt, cumin, cayenne pepper, and beans. Stir to combine ingredients. Bring to a boil, then reduce heat to low and simmer, uncovered, for 45 minutes, stirring occasionally. (Makes 8 cups.)

Freeze leftover chili in maxi muffins tins (approximately 1 cup measure). When frozen, pop chili out of tins and transfer to a freezer-weight zipper bag. Freeze until needed. Defrost these small portions as a quick topping for a baked potato, with shredded cheese and sour cream. Make nachos by topping a layer of tortilla chips with chili, chopped onions, sliced black olives, and shredded Mexican blend cheese. Or place chili and nacho ingredients atop a bowl of torn iceberg lettuce to create a taco salad. Transform a hot dog into a chili dog or ordinary French fries into chili fries. Add chili to a portion of instant Easy Mac macaroni and cheese to make Chili Mac.

Serves: 8 or 4 with leftovers.

Huevos Rancheros

The salsa is the key in this rendition of Spanish ranch-style eggs. Look for fresh, finely diced salsa or pico de gallo, packaged without a lot of liquid (drain liquid if necessary), or make your own fresh salsa. The chili is somewhat spicy, so choose the heat of the salsa — mild, medium, or hot — based on personal preferences.

1 small flour tortilla (6½-inch diameter)

¼ cup shredded sharp cheddar cheese

⅓ cup fresh salsa, drained of liquid

1 large egg

½ cup leftover Aunt Rita's Tried-and-True Two-Bean Chili

Salt and black pepper

1 tablespoon sour cream

2 tablespoons shredded lettuce

Preheat oven to 350°F. Place tortilla on a nonstick baking sheet. Bake for 2 minutes. Turn tortilla with tongs and bake for 2 minutes more. Spread cheese in an even layer atop tortilla and bake until cheese is melted, about 30 seconds.

Meanwhile, coat an 8-inch nonstick skillet with vegetable cooking oil. Place salsa in skillet, pressing with the back of spoon to form about a 5-inch circle. Press in the middle to form a slight indent. Cook on medium heat, covered, until salsa starts to sizzle, about 30 seconds. Break egg into a small bowl. Carefully transfer egg to center of salsa. Cover and cook egg until poached, 2 to 3 minutes. (Be sure not to overcook eggs.)

Reheat chili in a microwave-safe container on high for 1½ minutes.

To assemble: Place tortilla on dinner plate. Spread chili over tortilla. Transfer egg-topped salsa to tortilla with a firm spatula. Season egg with salt and pepper to taste. Top with sour cream and lettuce. Serve immediately.

To make 2 servings, use two 8-inch nonstick skillets and follow instructions above. For multiple servings, increase proportions accordingly. Use a large nonstick skillet to poach the eggs. Spread salsa in an even layer in the skillet. Place 2 eggs about 2 inches apart in the center of the salsa, then position remaining eggs around the perimeter. Carefully transfer eggs and a portion of the salsa to each of the cheese- and chili-topped tortillas.

Serves: 1

Knockoff Cincinnati Chili

The Skyline restaurant chain's famous entrée — Cincinnati Chili — is cherished by chili fans living in or just passing through the state of Ohio. It is always served over spaghetti, with a side of oyster crackers. Served "three-way" (topped with shredded cheddar cheese), "four-way" (topped with chopped onions or red beans), or "five-way" (topped with onions and red beans), the dish is legendary. A dash of Tabasco sauce finishes it (and you) off!

2 ounces dry spaghetti
½ cup leftover Aunt Rita's Tried-and-True Two-Bean Chili
¼ cup shredded sharp cheddar cheese
Oyster crackers

Bring a pot of water to boil over high heat. Add spaghetti and cook to al dente, following manufacturer's instructions, about 8 to 10 minutes. Drain spaghetti in colander and place on a dinner plate.

Meanwhile, reheat chili in a small saucepan over medium-low heat. Top spaghetti with chili. Sprinkle cheese over chili. Serve with a side portion of oyster crackers.

Increase proportions of ingredients depending on how many people you are serving. Although the chili used in this recipe already has onions and beans, you still can have Cincinnati Chili your way by topping it with raw chopped onions, red beans, and a dash of hot sauce before sprinkling cheese on top.

Serves: 1

Frito Pie

Called a Frito Boat by some, this Texas creation tastes a lot better than it sounds. For many, Frito Pie evokes distant memories of adolescence; it was a favorite at the concession stands and tailgating at football games in the Lone Star State. This is junk food at its best!

1 cup leftover Aunt Rita's Tried-and-True Two-Bean Chili
1 (3³/₈-ounce) bag Fritos brand corn chips
½ cup shredded cheddar cheese

Place chili in a microwavable bowl and reheat for 1 minute until heated through. Carefully cut open the Frito bag, lengthwise along the seam. Pour chili over Fritos. Sprinkle cheese atop chili. Mix chili with Fritos and cheese with a plastic fork and dig in.

An authentic Frito Pie has only the above 3 ingredients, but you can improvise by adding chopped raw onions and/or minced jalapeño peppers if you like. For a 1.75-ounce bag of Fritos, add ½ cup chili and ¼ cup cheese. To make Frito Pie for a crowd, use 4 cups Fritos, 2½ cups chili, and 2 cups cheese. In a 7x11-inch baking dish, layer Fritos, warm chili, cheese, Fritos, warm chili, and cheese. Bake at 350°F for 5 minutes or until cheese is melted.

Serves: 1

Grilled Asian Sirloin Steak

The secret to this succulent steak is the hoisin marinade. Be sure to allow steak to marinate at least 24 hours.

¼ cup hoisin sauce

2 tablespoons oyster sauce

3 tablespoons plum sauce

1 tablespoon Asian sweet chili sauce

2 tablespoons dry vermouth

1 tablespoon canola oil

1 tablespoon garlic paste or finely minced garlic

1 tablespoon gingerroot paste or finely minced gingerroot

2½ to 3 pounds sirloin steak, cut 1- to 1½-inch thick

At least 24 and up to 36 hours ahead: Mix hoisin, oyster, plum, and chili sauces together in a medium bowl. Stir in vermouth, canola oil, garlic, and gingerroot. Place sirloin in a large, freezer-weight zipper bag. Pour marinade into bag. Seal bag and massage marinade into steak. Refrigerate until needed.

To grill: Preheat gas grill to 450°F. Remove steak from marinade and transfer marinade to a small microwave-safe bowl. Microwave marinade for 1 minute. Place steak on the grill and baste with marinade. Grill for 6 minutes. Turn steak and baste with marinade. Continue cooking until steak is medium-rare, about 6 to 8 minutes longer.

Remove steak from grill and cut across the grain into ⅜-inch slices.

You can substitute white wine for the dry vermouth in this recipe. You'll find hoisin, oyster, plum, and sweet Asian chili sauces in the Asian food section of your supermarket.

Serves: 6

Asian Steak, Cantaloupe, and Brie Quesadillas

An unlikely combination, the ingredients in these quesadillas cross borders to create a unique cultural flavor fusion.

4 (10-inch) flour tortillas
¼ cup fruit-flavored honey mustard
¼ pound leftover Grilled Asian Sirloin Steak slices, cut into thin pieces
¼ cup chopped red onions
1 cup thinly sliced cantaloupe
4 ounces Brie, thinly sliced
2 teaspoons snipped fresh cilantro (optional)
1 tablespoon butter, divided

Place 2 tortillas on kitchen counter. Spread 2 tablespoons honey mustard evenly over each of the tortillas. Place half the steak slices, half the red onions, and half the sliced cantaloupe evenly over each tortilla. Divide the Brie evenly between the two tortillas. Sprinkle 1 teaspoon cilantro on each tortilla. Place one of the remaining 2 tortillas atop each layered tortilla.

Place a 12-inch nonstick skillet over medium-high heat. Melt ½ tablespoon butter in skillet until bubbly. Slide 1 quesadilla onto a pizza sheet. Slide quesadilla from sheet into skillet. Place a 10-inch skillet atop quesadilla and cook for 2 minutes or until underside is golden.

Remove top skillet, place pizza sheet atop 12-inch skillet, and flip quesadilla onto pizza sheet. Slide flipped quesadilla into skillet. Top with 10-inch skillet and cook for 2 minutes more, until underside is golden. Slide quesadilla onto cutting board.

Repeat this procedure with remaining quesadilla. Cut each quesadilla into 6 wedges with a pizza cutter and serve immediately.

Substitute grilled pork tenderloin or chicken for sirloin steak, thinly sliced apples or peaches for cantaloupe. I used cherry honey mustard, but any fruit-flavored honey mustard will work. The best are those mustards found at fruit stands or gourmet food stores.

Serves: 4 (3 wedges each)

Thai Beef Salad

The Asian-marinated steak works perfectly in this beef salad, a staple in Thai cuisine. Don't be wary of the fish sauce. It certainly does smell fishy, but its unique flavor is essential to all Thai dishes.

1½ teaspoons crushed garlic or garlic paste

1 tablespoon fish sauce

1 tablespoon sugar

2 tablespoons fresh lime juice

¾ pound Grilled Asian Sirloin Steak slices, cut into ¼-inch strips

2 tablespoons snipped fresh cilantro

1 tablespoon snipped fresh mint

2 teaspoons finely minced jalapeño peppers

4 cups mixed greens, torn into bite-size pieces

2 plum tomatoes, thinly sliced

½ cup thinly sliced English cucumber

¼ cup thinly sliced red onions

½ cup thinly sliced red bell pepper

At least 4 hours and up to 8 hours ahead: Whisk together garlic, fish sauce, sugar, and lime juice in a small bowl. Set aside. Place steak strips, cilantro, mint, and jalapeño peppers in a medium covered container. Toss to mix. Pour lime juice mixture over steak mixture and toss until steak is well coated with dressing. Cover and refrigerate until needed.

To serve: Place mixed greens on a serving platter. Arrange tomato slices, cucumbers, onions, and bell peppers in layers atop greens. Remove beef strips from dressing with a slotted spoon and place atop vegetables. Drizzle remaining dressing over vegetables and greens.

Serve with freshly baked bread sticks. You'll find fish sauce in the Asian section of your supermarket.

Serves: 4 for lunch; 2 for dinner

South African Flank Steak Braai

What the grill is to Americans and the barbie is to Australians, so is the braai to South Africans. Indonesian flavors firmly entrenched in Cape Town history and cuisine make their way to meats cooked over the outdoor fire.

¼ cup olive oil

1 cup chopped sweet onions, like Vidalia

1 teaspoon garlic paste or finely minced garlic

⅜ teaspoon chili powder

1 tablespoon peanut butter

2 teaspoons ground turmeric

1 tablespoon brown sugar

3 tablespoons soy sauce

1 tablespoon fresh lemon juice

¾ cup water

1½ pounds flank steak

At least 2 hours or up to 12 hours ahead: Off heat, mix oil, onions, garlic, chili powder, peanut butter, turmeric, brown sugar, soy sauce, lemon juice, and water together in a nonstick medium saucepan. Place saucepan over medium-low heat and bring to a simmer. Simmer, uncovered, for 5 minutes. Remove from heat and allow marinade to cool.

Shallowly score both sides of flank steak in a cross-hatch pattern with a sharp knife. Place meat in a large freezer-weight zipper bag. Pour marinade over meat, close bag, and refrigerate for at least 2 hours.

To grill: Heat a gas grill to high. Remove steak from marinade. Microwave marinade for 1 minute. Grill flank steak for 3 minutes per side. Remove from grill and slice thinly on the diagonal. (Meat will be rare, but will keep cooking after it is sliced, becoming medium-rare.) Serve meat with marinade sauce on the side.

Flank steak is as tender and flavorful as more expensive cuts of meat if prepared properly. Scoring and marinating for at least several hours, then grilling to rare and slicing the steak on the diagonal guarantees success.

Serves: 6 or 4 with leftovers

Blue Cheese Steak Bites

Easy to prepare, these tasty bites are perfect for a light lunch or a heavy hors d'oeuvre.

½ bread baguette, cut into ¼-inch slices on the diagonal (14 slices)

Olive oil spray

⅓ cup mayonnaise

⅓ cup crumbled blue cheese

¼ teaspoon dry mustard

2 teaspoons white wine vinegar

½ cup finely chopped seeded plum tomatoes

¼ cup finely chopped red onions

2 tablespoons snipped fresh basil plus 3 whole basil leaves

¼ teaspoon salt

2 teaspoons extra-virgin olive oil

4 ounces leftover sliced South African Flank Steak Braai, cut into very small pieces

Up to I hour ahead: Preheat oven to 425°F. Place baguette slices on a nonstick baking sheet. Coat with olive oil spray. Bake for 2 to 4 minutes, until toasted but not hard. Remove from oven.

Meanwhile, mix mayonnaise, blue cheese, dry mustard, and vinegar together in a small bowl. Set aside. Mix tomatoes, onions, 2 tablespoons snipped basil, salt, and olive oil in a medium bowl. Allow flavors to marry for 10 to 15 minutes.

To serve: Add flank steak pieces to tomato mixture and toss to combine. Spread blue cheese mixture generously on toasted baguette slices. Top each baguette slice with an equal portion of the steak and tomato mixture. Roll the 3 remaining basil pieces into a tight cylinder. Snip cylinder, crosswise, into very thin strips using kitchen scissors. Unroll basil strips and sprinkle an equal amount over each Steak Bite. Place on a glass platter and serve.

Adjust proportions in this recipe depending upon how much leftover flank steak you have.

Makes: 14 Steak Bites

Beef on a Weck Sandwich

Indigenous to western New York state and western Pennsylvania, this sandwich is legendary in its simplicity and its taste. The weck is a kummelweck roll, a Kaiser-shaped roll topped with coarse salt and caraway seeds. The roll is filled with thinly sliced rare beef topped with horseradish sauce.

2 Kaiser or knot rolls

Olive oil spray

½ teaspoon coarse kosher salt

1 teaspoon caraway seeds

5 ounces leftover rare South African Flank Steak Braai slices

⅓ cup Horseradish Cream Sauce (recipe page 33)

Preheat oven to 350°F. Coat tops of rolls with olive oil spray. Sprinkle each roll with ¼ teaspoon salt and ½ teaspoon caraway seeds. Place rolls on a nonstick baking sheet and bake for 5 minutes. Place beef in a microwavable container. Reheat in microwave for 30 seconds.

Cut rolls in half. Place 2½ ounces beef on the bottom half of each roll. Divide horseradish sauce between the 2 rolls, spreading generously on the cut side of the tops. Put tops and bottoms of sandwiches together, cut each sandwich in half, and serve immediately.

An authentic weck sandwich is made with thinly sliced rare roast beef tenderloin, prime rib, or eye of the round. The beef is dipped in au jus before it is placed on the bun. If you are planning to serve these sandwiches from grilled flank, you can save the au jus you'll get from slicing the steak.

Serves: 2

Fancy Schmancy Meat Loaf with Cranberry Ketchup

Invest in a molded loaf pan to turn everyday meat loaf into a company meal. The Nordic Ware Fancy Bundt Loaf Pan has a nonstick interior finish and makes a great baking pan for breakfast breads as well.

3 pounds ground beef (90 percent lean)

½ cup finely chopped sweet onions, like Vidalia

¾ cup raisins

¼ cup dried parsley

¾ teaspoon dry mustard

1½ tablespoons Parmesan cheese

2¼ teaspoons dried oregano

1½ teaspoons salt

⅜ teaspoon white pepper

⅜ teaspoon ground coriander

1 tablespoon garlic paste or finely minced garlic

3 eggs, beaten

3 cups Japanese-style panko bread crumbs

½ cup pine nuts

5 tablespoons Cranberry Ketchup, plus more for serving (recipe page 112)

Preheat oven to 350°F. Place beef, onions, raisins, parsley, dry mustard, Parmesan cheese, oregano, salt, pepper, coriander, and garlic in a large bowl. With clean hands, mix ingredients together well. Using the same method, mix in eggs, then bread crumbs and pine nuts. Transfer meatloaf mixture to a 10-cup loaf pan that has been coated with vegetable cooking spray. Press mixture firmly into the pan, filling all crevices.

Bake meat loaf, uncovered, for 1 hour. Spread Cranberry Ketchup atop meat loaf. Return meat loaf to oven and bake 15 minutes more. Gently remove meat loaf from the pan with 2 firm spatulas and place on a serving platter. Slice and serve with additional Cranberry Ketchup on the side.

Once assembled, you can cover the meat loaf with plastic wrap and then a double layer of aluminum foil and freeze until needed. Divide meat loaf mixture among smaller pans if you like. Adjust cooking time accordingly.

Serves: 10 to 12 or 4 to 6 with leftovers

Spicy Meat Loaf–Mushroom Lasagna

This hearty lasagna will feed a crowd. Or you can divide the recipe between two deep lasagna pans and refrigerate one for dinner tonight or tomorrow night and freeze one to use another time.

1 tablespoon olive oil

3 teaspoons garlic paste or finely minced garlic

1 cup chopped sweet onions, like Vidalia

1 pound button mushrooms, chopped

1 tablespoon red wine

1 (28-ounce) can crushed tomatoes

2 (14.5-ounce) cans diced tomatoes with basil, garlic, and oregano

1 teaspoon crushed red pepper flakes

½ teaspoon dried oregano

1 tablespoon dried basil

1 teaspoon dried marjoram

½ teaspoon sugar

½ teaspoon salt

1 (9-ounce) box flat no-cook lasagna noodles

1 (16-ounce) carton part-skim ricotta cheese

1 (16-ounce) package shredded mozzarella cheese

2 pounds leftover Fancy Schmancy Meat Loaf, thinly sliced (a little less than half the original meat loaf)

1 cup grated Parmesan cheese

Early in the day or I day ahead: Heat oil in a large nonstick saucepan over medium heat. Add garlic and onions. Sauté, stirring frequently, until onions are soft, about 2 minutes. Reduce heat to medium-low. Add mushrooms and wine. Cook for 5 minutes, stirring occasionally. Reduce heat to low. Add crushed tomatoes and diced tomatoes. Cover and simmer for 15 minutes, stirring occasionally. Stir in red pepper flakes, oregano, basil, marjoram, sugar, and salt. Simmer sauce, covered, for 20 more minutes.

Spread 1½ cups sauce in the bottom of a 13x10x4-inch-deep aluminum lasagna pan. Place a layer of lasagna noodles atop sauce. Spread ½ cup ricotta cheese over noodles. Sprinkle 1½ cups mozzarella over ricotta. Place a layer of meat loaf atop mozzarella.

Repeat layering using measurements above: sauce, noodles, ricotta, mozzarella, meat loaf, sauce, noodles, ricotta, mozzarella. Top with remaining sauce and sprinkle with Parmesan cheese. Cover with aluminum foil and refrigerate until needed.

To bake: Preheat oven to 350°F. Bake lasagna, covered, for 1 hour. Remove foil and bake for 30 minutes more, until lasagna is bubbly and heated through.

If you don't have 2 pounds meat loaf left over, adjust proportions for lasagna noodles and cheeses accordingly. You can make the mushroom marinara sauce as instructed above. Freeze whatever you don't use and serve it atop spaghetti, penne, or ravioli for another meal.

Serves: 10 to 12

Red Currant-glazed Corned Beef

You'll never think "boiled dinner" again, once you've tasted this company-quality corned beef. Serve with Salt-crusted Baked New Potatoes (recipe page 94).

½ cup brown sugar, divided

1 teaspoon dry mustard

½ teaspoon black pepper

½ teaspoon ground cloves

1 4-pound flat-cut corned beef, rinsed and dried

1 tablespoon cider vinegar

1 tablespoon mint sauce or 2 sprigs fresh mint leaves

2 cups apple juice

1 (12-ounce) jar red currant jelly (1 cup)

¼ cup Dijon mustard

Early in the day: Mix 2 tablespoons brown sugar, dry mustard, pepper, and cloves together in a small bowl. Rub mixture into both sides of corned beef. Place corned beef in a slow cooker.

Mix 2 tablespoons brown sugar, vinegar, mint sauce, and apple juice in a medium bowl. Pour mixture over corned beef. Add water so that corned beef is just barely covered. Cook on high for 1 hour. Reduce heat to low and cook in slow cooker for 8 hours.

To finish: Preheat oven to 350°F. Remove corned beef from slow cooker (discard liquid) and place in a shallow baking pan that has been coated with vegetable cooking spray. Whisk ¼ cup brown sugar, red currant jelly, and mustard together in a medium bowl. Pour glaze mixture over corned beef. Bake, uncovered, for 30 minutes. Spoon glaze (pooled in bottom of pan) atop corned beef. Bake for 15 minutes more.

Slice corned beef across grain into ½-inch slices. Transfer remaining glaze into a small pitcher. Serve as sauce with corned beef.

If you don't want to cook corned beef in a slow cooker, place corned beef and cooking liquids in a large pot over high heat. Bring to a boil. Reduce heat to low, cover, and simmer for 3 hours, until tender. Then proceed with glazing and baking instructions above.

Serves: 8 or 4 with leftovers

Corned Beef Hash

Traditionally, hash is served topped with a fried or poached egg for breakfast or brunch. Make this a dinner item by topping it with a tossed green salad.

4 tablespoons butter

1 cup chopped sweet onions, like Vidalia

1 teaspoon garlic paste or finely minced garlic

2 cups finely chopped leftover Red Currant-glazed Corned Beef

2 cups finely chopped leftover Salt-crusted Baked New Potatoes (recipe page 94)

½ cup chopped green bell peppers

¼ teaspoon salt

¼ teaspoon black pepper

¼ cup snipped fresh curly parsley

Melt butter in a large nonstick skillet over medium heat. Add onions and garlic and sauté for 1 minute, stirring constantly. Add corned beef and potatoes. Reduce heat to medium-low and sauté, stirring frequently for 3 minutes. Add bell peppers and cook for 2 minutes more, stirring frequently. Stir in parsley and serve immediately or refrigerate or freeze until needed.

You can refrigerate (up to 2 days) or freeze hash (up to 2 weeks) for use at another time. Reheat defrosted hash in a skillet over low heat for 2 to 3 minutes, stirring frequently, until heated through.

Serves: 4 to 6

Herb-marinated Grill-roasted Boneless Leg of Lamb

Boneless leg of lamb has been deboned, butterflied, and rolled into a roast that is held together by a web of netting. You can leave the netting on the roast for grilling. Cut it off with a kitchen scissors before carving.

½ cup white balsamic vinegar

3 tablespoons snipped fresh mint or 1 tablespoon dried

2 tablespoons snipped fresh thyme or 2 teaspoons dried

1 tablespoon snipped fresh oregano or 1 teaspoon dried

2 tablespoons snipped fresh rosemary or 2 teaspoons dried

10 cloves garlic, divided

1 teaspoon cracked black pepper

1 cup olive oil

1 (4-pound) boneless leg of lamb

At least 8 hours and up to 24 hours ahead: Place vinegar, mint, thyme, oregano, rosemary, 2 garlic cloves, and pepper in a blender. Pulse to puree. With blender at low speed, slowly add olive oil. Set aside.

Cut remaining 8 garlic cloves into slivers. Randomly puncture lamb with the tip of a sharp knife. Insert a garlic sliver into each cut. Place lamb in a large zipper bag. Pour marinade over lamb. Close bag and massage marinade into lamb until it is completely covered. Refrigerate until needed, turning bag and massaging marinade into lamb occasionally.

Preheat gas grill to 425°F. Remove lamb from marinade. Bring to room temperature. Grill lamb for 1 hour, 15 minutes (about 18 minutes per pound). Test internal temperature with an instant-read thermometer (135° for medium-rare). Cut meat across the grain into ½-inch slices.

Lamb will continue cooking about 5 degrees after it has been removed from the grill. For medium-rare, take roast off grill at an internal temperature of 130 degrees.

Serves: 8 or 4 with leftovers

Middle Eastern–style Lamb Penne Pasta

Lamb seasoned with coriander and cumin is a classic combination in many countries of the Middle East and Med Rim, although it would always be served with rice, never pasta. The collision of cultures in this recipe fuses flavors of several cuisines.

Salt

1 pound penne rigate pasta

1 tablespoon olive oil

1 cup chopped sweet onions, like Vidalia

2 teaspoons garlic paste or minced garlic

2 teaspoons gingerroot paste or minced gingerroot

1 (14.5-ounce) can petite-diced tomatoes in garlic and oil, with juices

½ cup water

1½ teaspoons ground coriander

¾ teaspoon ground cumin

¼ teaspoon crushed red pepper flakes

½ pound leftover Herb-marinated Grill-roasted Boneless Lamb, cut into ¼-inch dice

2 tablespoons snipped fresh cilantro

¼ cup plain yogurt

Place a large pot of water over high heat. Add 1 tablespoon salt and bring to a boil. Add penne, reduce heat to medium, and cook pasta until al dente according to manufacturer's instructions, about 10 minutes. Drain in a colander.

Meanwhile, place oil in a large nonstick skillet over medium heat. Add onions and sauté, stirring frequently, for 2 minutes. Add garlic and gingerroot and cook for 1 minute, stirring constantly.

Reduce heat to low. Add tomatoes, water, coriander, cumin, red pepper flakes, and 1 teaspoon salt. Cook for 3 minutes, stirring frequently. Add diced lamb and cilantro. Cook for 5 minutes more, stirring frequently, until lamb has heated through and mixture is bubbly. Add pasta and toss to combine. Transfer pasta mixture to 4 individual pasta bowls. Top each serving with 1 tablespoon yogurt and serve immediately.

Penne is a great pasta choice in this recipe. Its tubular structure traps the sauce's small tidbits of lamb and tomato.

Serves: 4

Shepherd's Pie

A fine English tradition, shepherd's pie is so named because it is made with lamb. If you were to use beef, it would be called cottage pie.

1 tablespoon butter

1 tablespoon garlic paste or finely minced garlic

4 ounces button mushrooms, thinly sliced (about 1 heaping cup)

1 sweet onion, like Vidalia, thinly sliced and quartered (about 1 heaping cup)

1 tablespoon flour

¼ cup white wine

1 cup beef broth

1 tablespoon tomato paste

½ pound baby carrots, quartered lengthwise and halved crosswise (about 1½ cups)

1 red bell pepper, sliced and cut into 1-inch slivers (about 1 heaping cup)

½ teaspoon salt

¼ teaspoon black pepper

½ teaspoon thyme

1 pound leftover Herb-marinated Grill-roasted Boneless Lamb, cut into bite-size pieces

3½ cups leftover Mashed Potato Gratin (recipe page 96)

¼ cup half-and-half

Melt butter in a large nonstick skillet over medium heat. Add garlic, mushrooms, and onions. Sauté until onions are soft and mushroom liquid has evaporated, about 2 minutes.

Reduce heat to low. Stir in flour. Gradually add wine and broth, stirring constantly. Stir in tomato paste. Add carrots, bell peppers, salt, pepper, and thyme. Cover and simmer for 5 minutes, until carrots are al dente. Add lamb and cook, uncovered, stirring frequently, for 5 minutes more, until lamb is heated through.

Coat a deep-dish pie plate with vegetable cooking spray. Transfer lamb and vegetable mixture to pie plate. Place leftover mashed potatoes in a microwave-safe bowl and reheat for 2 minutes. Stir in half-and-half. Spread mashed potatoes atop lamb mixture, to the outer rim of pie plate, sealing lamb and juices beneath. Create a decorative pattern in mashed potatoes with the tines of a fork. Cover pie with plastic wrap and aluminum foil and refrigerate or freeze until needed.

To bake: Preheat oven to 375°F. Bring pie to room temperature. Remove plastic wrap and aluminum foil. Place pie on a baking sheet. Bake for 30 to 40 minutes, until mixture is bubbly and has heated through.

You can freeze this pie for up to 1 month. You can substitute an equal amount of cooked ground beef for the lamb to create a cottage pie.

Serves: 6

Sesame-seared Yellowfin Tuna with Ponzu Sauce

Ponzu sauce is a sweet, sour, slightly salty sauce commonly used in Japanese cuisine. Drizzle it sparingly over the rare tuna.

2 tablespoons fresh lemon juice

1 tablespoon fresh orange juice

2 tablespoons mirin

3 tablespoons soy sauce

1 teaspoon toasted sesame oil

1 teaspoon cornstarch

¼ cup white sesame seeds

1 tablespoon black sesame seeds

¼ teaspoon freshly ground black pepper

1 teaspoon cracked black pepper

1 teaspoon kosher salt

2 pounds yellowfin tuna steaks, cut 1-inch thick

Olive oil spray

Mix together lemon and orange juices, mirin, soy sauce, and sesame oil in a small nonstick saucepan. Place cornstarch in a small bowl. Whisk in 1 teaspoon juice mixture until smooth. Place saucepan over medium heat. When sauce comes to a boil, reduce heat to low. Whisk in cornstarch mixture until sauce has thickened slightly, about 30 seconds. Remove from heat. Reheat gently on low before serving.

Mix together sesame seeds, ground and cracked pepper, and salt in a small bowl. Transfer to a shallow dish. Press both sides and edges of tuna into sesame seed mixture so that seeds adhere to the fish. Coat sesame seeds with olive oil spray.

Preheat a gas grill to hottest setting. Sear tuna for 2 minutes on each side. Remove tuna from heat and cut into ⅜-inch slices. Serve tuna drizzled with Ponzu Sauce.

Mirin is a sweet Japanese rice cooking wine. You'll find it in the Asian food section of your supermarket.

Serves: 6 or 4 with leftovers

Yellowfin Tuna Tacos

Seared rare tuna is just too good to cook any further. These soft tortilla tacos make the most of leftover tuna, enhancing its flavor with a spicy sour cream sauce and an array of cooling condiments.

½ cup chopped red onions
1 cup sour cream, divided
¼ cup snipped fresh cilantro
½ teaspoon chipotle chile powder
Olive oil spray
6 (8-inch) flour tortillas
8 ounces leftover Sesame-seared Yellowfin Tuna, cut into bite-size pieces
⅓ cup guacamole
½ cup chunky mild fresh mango salsa
1 (2.25-ounce) can sliced black olives, drained
1 cup shredded pepper jack cheese
1 cup chiffonade-cut romaine lettuce tops

Stir onions, ⅔ cup sour cream, cilantro, and chipolte chile powder together in a small saucepan. Place saucepan over medium-low heat, stirring frequently. Cook just until sauce is heated through, about 2 minutes.

Place a medium nonstick skillet over medium-low heat. For each tortilla: Coat skillet with olive oil spray. Place tortilla in skillet. Coat top of tortilla with olive oil spray. Cook for 20 seconds. Turn tortilla over with tongs and cook 20 seconds more. Transfer tortilla to a plate and cover with aluminum foil.

Remove warm sour cream sauce from heat and stir in tuna pieces. Divide sauced tuna equally, placing it across the middle of each of the 6 tortillas. Place guacamole, salsa, olives, cheese, lettuce, and ⅓ cup sour cream in small serving bowls. Allow diners to top their tuna tacos with their choice of any or all condiments.

Fold tortilla burrito-style, like an envelope, to keep all the great ingredients inside. You can substitute shredded cabbage for the lettuce for a little more crunch. If you don't have chipotle chile powder, you can substitute 1 teaspoon minced canned chipotle chiles.

Serves: 3

Tuna Salad Melt

Make up this fresh tuna salad a couple of hours ahead so that the tuna soaks up the Asian flavors of the sauce. Add the mayonnaise just before serving. This sandwich makes a hearty lunch or, when served with a salad, a light dinner.

3 scallions, chopped

2 tablespoons chopped shallots

1 teaspoon gingerroot paste or finely minced gingerroot

2 tablespoons chopped peanuts

½ teaspoon crushed red pepper flakes

2 tablespoons snipped fresh cilantro

3 tablespoons fresh lime juice

2 tablespoons fish sauce

8 ounces leftover Sesame-seared Yellowfin Tuna

2 Kaiser rolls

⅓ cup mayonnaise

6 thin slices Swiss cheese

Up to 2 hours ahead: Mix together scallions, shallots, gingerroot, peanuts, red pepper flakes, cilantro, lime juice, and fish sauce in a medium bowl.

Cut tuna slices in half lengthwise, then cut into ½-inch dice. Add to scallion mixture and toss to combine. Cover bowl with plastic wrap and refrigerate until ready to serve.

To bake: Preheat oven to 375°F. Cut rolls in half horizontally. Add mayonnaise to tuna mixture and toss until ingredients are well coated. Spread half the tuna mixture on the bottom half of each roll (reserve tops for another use). Top each roll with 3 slices of cheese, positioned so that when melted, cheese will encase the tuna.

Place rolls on a baking sheet and bake for 3 minutes, until cheese has melted. Cut each tuna-topped roll in half and serve immediately.

For a protein-packed breakfast, toast the reserved tops of the Kaiser rolls in the morning. Place a layer of thinly sliced tomatoes and a layer of Swiss cheese atop each half roll and microwave for 20 seconds, until cheese is soft and starts to melt.

Serves: 2

Soy-Ginger Salmon Fillets Roasted on Potato Galettes

Traditionally galettes are round, flat French cakes. In this recipe, thin potato slices are overlapped to form a circular nest upon which to roast the salmon fillets.

2½ pounds Yukon Gold or other yellow potatoes
Olive oil spray
Salt and freshly ground black pepper
½ cup soy sauce
1 tablespoon plus 1 teaspoon gingerroot paste or finely minced gingerroot
¼ cup honey
¼ cup Dijon mustard
1 tablespoon plus 1 teaspoon grated orange peel
4 (4.5- to 5-ounce) wild Alaskan sockeye or king salmon fillets, skin removed
2 tablespoons snipped fresh parsley

Preheat oven to 400°F. Peel potatoes and cut into very thin slices. Coat 2 nonstick baking sheets with olive oil spray. Working one at a time, create 4 galettes: Place potato slices in a 6-inch circle, overlapping slices and filling in the center with an overlapping layer. Coat galettes with olive oil spray. Season with salt and pepper to taste. Bake for 30 minutes. Remove from oven.

Meanwhile, mix soy sauce, gingerroot, honey, mustard, and orange peel together in a medium bowl. Rinse salmon fillets and pat dry with paper toweling. Place fillets in a shallow container. Pour soy sauce mixture over fillets, then spoon mixture over fillets so that all surfaces are coated. Refrigerate for 15 minutes.

Place 1 salmon fillet atop each potato galette. Spoon sauce over fillets, taking care that it doesn't drip down onto potatoes. Place in the oven and roast for 10 to 12 minutes, until salmon is barely cooked through. Remove from oven. (Salmon will continue to cook when removed from oven.) Place 1 salmon-topped galette on each dinner plate, using a firm spatula. Sprinkle ½ tablespoon snipped parsley atop salmon and serve immediately.

Summer is the season you'll find fresh Alaskan sockeye or king salmon at your fishmonger or your supermarket. The other months of the year, the wild salmon offered has been flash-frozen in Alaska, then defrosted at the market. To guarantee your salmon fillets haven't been sitting, defrosted, in the display case for several days, ask for a whole frozen fillet, which will feed four. If you want only 2 portions, heat a paring knife under hot water repeatedly and cut fillet in half, using the point of the hot knife. Defrost one half and place remainder of frozen salmon in the freezer.

Serves: 4 or 2 to 3 with leftovers

Dilled Fish Spread Sandwiches

Tastier than canned tuna fish sandwiches, this is a great way to use up any leftover fish, such as grouper, snapper, flounder, cod, walleye, or tilapia.

1¼ cups leftover Soy-Ginger Salmon Fillets, flaked

2 tablespoons chopped sweet onions, such as Vidalia

¼ cup commercially prepared dill dip

Freshly ground black pepper

8 slices bread, lightly toasted

1 tomato, thinly sliced

Mix flaked fish, onions, and dill dip together in a medium bowl. Add ground pepper to taste.

Spread a quarter of the fish mixture over each of 4 toast slices. Top each with thinly sliced tomato and a second piece of toast.

If Friday night fish fries are de rigeur in your neighborhood, bring home your "doggie bag" of leftovers. Remove breading before flaking. Use any mixture of leftover grilled, fried, sautéed, or baked fish. You can freeze leftover bits from multiple meals until you have enough fish to make the spread. Simply defrost fish in the refrigerator and proceed with the recipe above. You can serve this fish spread with crackers for a tasty hors d'oeuvre as well.

Serves: 6

Grilled Marinated Swordfish

The marinade gives this swordfish the grilled cross-hatch marks you'd find in a fine seafood restaurant. If your grill doesn't have a thermostat, just use the hottest setting.

2 tablespoons soy sauce

¼ cup orange juice

2 tablespoons ketchup

2 tablespoons snipped fresh flat-leaf parsley

1 tablespoon fresh lemon juice

½ teaspoon black pepper

1 teaspoon garlic paste or finely minced garlic

2 pounds fresh swordfish, cut 1½ inches thick

Two hours ahead: Mix soy sauce, orange juice, ketchup, parsley, lemon juice, pepper, and garlic together in a medium bowl. Rinse swordfish and dry with paper toweling. Pour half the marinade in a shallow dish. Place swordfish atop marinade. Pour remaining marinade over swordfish. Cover and refrigerate until needed.

To grill: Preheat gas grill to 550°F (hot grill). Remove swordfish from marinade. Place marinade in a microwave-safe container and heat for 1 minute. Place swordfish on grill. Brush with marinade. Grill swordfish for 5½ minutes. Turn swordfish and brush with marinade. Grill for 5½ minutes more. (Fish should have just lost its translucency; do not overcook or fish will be dry.) Brush with marinade before serving. Serve immediately.

You can use this marinade on other fish as well. But if using a flaky white fish, marinate the fish for no more than 30 minutes. Adjust grilling time according to the thickness of the fish.

Serves: 4 or 2 with leftovers

Louise's Cantonese Fish and Vegetable Soup

Louise lives in the Florida Keys with her fishing guide husband, so she's an expert at "fishy" transformations. This easy recipe is a winner!

1 cup dried sliced shiitake mushrooms
½ tablespoon canola oil
½ cup quartered and thinly sliced onions
1½ teaspoons garlic paste or finely minced garlic
1½ tablespoons gingerroot paste or finely minced gingerroot
1 cup 1-inch-long matchstick-cut carrots
¼ cup soy sauce
3 tablespoons cornstarch
2 teaspoons toasted sesame oil
3 big dashes bottled hot sauce
12 ounces leftover Grilled Marinated Swordfish
⅓ cup diced roasted red bell peppers

Place dried mushrooms in a medium bowl and cover with ¾ cup boiling water. Set aside for 10 minutes.

Meanwhile, place canola oil in a large soup pot over medium heat. Add onions, garlic, and gingerroot, and sauté for 1 minute. Add carrots and cook for 1 minute, stirring constantly. Add mushrooms with soaking liquid and 4½ cups water to soup pot. Cover and bring to a boil.

Whisk together soy sauce, cornstarch, sesame oil, hot sauce, and 4½ tablespoons water in a small bowl. When soup comes to a boil, add cornstarch mixture. Reduce heat to low and cook, stirring occasionally, until soup is bubbly and thickens slightly. Cut swordfish into ¼-inch slices, then cut slices into ½-inch pieces. Add roasted red peppers and swordfish to soup. Stir gently and cook for 1 to 2 minutes, until fish is heated through.

You can use any firm-fleshed grilled fish for this recipe. If using salmon or a white fish like grouper or snapper, flake the fish with a fork instead of trying to slice it. If you can't find or don't have dried shiitake mushrooms, you can substitute thinly sliced baby bella or button mushrooms, but the flavor of the soup will be slightly altered.

Serves: 4

Shrimp and Brie Penne

Simply oozing with Brie, this shrimp dish rates as decadent company fare. Use leftovers to make a simple, savory shrimp and pasta soup (recipe follows).

1 cup julienne-cut sun-dried tomatoes

¾ cup snipped fresh basil

4 tomatoes, thickly sliced and cut into bite-size pieces

3 cloves garlic, finely minced

1 pound Brie cheese, rind removed and cut into bite-size pieces

½ teaspoon black pepper

½ teaspoon salt

⅔ cup plus 1 tablespoon light olive oil, divided

1 pound dried penne

1½ pounds jumbo shrimp (16/20s), peeled and deveined

1 teaspoon lemon-dill or lemon-pepper seasoning

Three hours ahead: Place sun-dried tomatoes, basil, chopped tomatoes, garlic, Brie, pepper, salt, and ⅔ cup olive oil in a large covered container. Toss to mix well. Cover container and refrigerate for 2 hours so that flavors marry. Stir mixture occasionally.

One hour ahead: Place tomato mixture in a large bowl and allow it to reach room temperature. Stir occasionally.

To cook: Bring a large pot of water to boil over high heat. When water comes to a full boil, add pasta. Stir to mix. When water returns to a boil, reduce heat to medium-high and cook pasta to al dente, following package instructions, about 10 minutes. Stir occasionally so pasta doesn't stick to bottom of pan. Drain pasta in a colander.

Meanwhile, place 1 tablespoon olive oil in a large nonstick skillet over medium-high heat. When oil is hot, add shrimp, season with lemon-dill or lemon-pepper, and sauté, stirring constantly, until shrimp are pink and just cooked through. Remove shrimp from heat.

Add shrimp and drained, hot pasta to tomato mixture. Toss to mix well. Divide pasta among 6 individual pasta bowls. Serve immediately.

Pre-julienne-cut sun-dried tomatoes are often available in the produce section of your supermarket. You'll find lemon-dill seasoning in gourmet markets that sell unusual seasoning blends. You can substitute the more common lemon-pepper seasoning if you can't find lemon-dill.

Serves: 6 or 4 with leftovers

Shrimp and Brie Penne Soup

This tasty soup couldn't be easier. Ready in fewer than 10 minutes, all the seasonings are packed into the leftover Shrimp and Brie Penne.

4 extra-large Knorr vegetable bouillon cubes or 8 cups vegetable broth
3 cups leftover Shrimp and Brie Penne (more is fine)
Parmesan cheese

Bring 8 cups water to boil over high heat. When water boils, add bouillon cubes and stir until they are dissolved. (If using vegetable broth, bring to a boil over high heat.) Reduce heat to low. Cut leftover shrimp into small bite-size pieces. Add shrimp and penne mixture to vegetable broth. Stir to combine. Simmer for 10 minutes, until heated through. Serve immediately or divide into 2 covered containers and refrigerate for up to 2 days or freeze for up to 1 month. Defrost and gently reheat on low before serving. Top each serving with a sprinkling of Parmesan cheese.

🍳 This recipe assumes that two servings or one-third of pasta mixture is leftover from original recipe. If you have more or less shrimp and pasta leftover, adjust amount of vegetable broth accordingly.

Makes: 12 cups

Barbecued Jumbo Shrimp

Jumbo shrimp are called 10/15s, because there are usually 10 to 15 shrimp to a pound. Meatier than most shrimp, they are the perfect size for grilling.

¼ cup chopped sweet onions, like Vidalia

½ cup ketchup

1 tablespoon brown sugar

1 tablespoon dry mustard

¼ teaspoon garlic powder

1 tablespoon white vinegar

2¼ pounds jumbo shrimp (10/15s), peeled and deveined

1 lemon, cut into 8 wedges

One hour ahead: Coat a small nonstick skillet with vegetable cooking spray. Place over medium heat. Add onions and sauté for 1 minute, stirring constantly. Remove skillet from heat. Stir in ketchup, brown sugar, dry mustard, garlic powder, and vinegar.

Rinse shrimp and pat them dry with paper toweling. Place shrimp in a covered container. Pour barbecue sauce over shrimp and toss shrimp until all are well coated with sauce. Cover and refrigerate for 1 hour.

To grill: Preheat gas grill to medium (about 400°). Coat 4 large metal skewers with vegetable cooking spray. Thread shrimp onto skewers, tail to top. Place barbecue sauce in a microwave-safe container. Heat in microwave for 1 minute on high. Grill shrimp skewers for 5 minutes. Turn skewers over and baste with barbecue sauce. Grill another 5 minutes, just until shrimp have lost their translucency when tested with a knife. Remove shrimp from skewers and place in a serving bowl. Serve immediately with lemon wedges.

You'll have about 30 to 32 shrimp with the poundage indicated above. Figure about 5 shrimp per person. Serve shrimp with a tossed salad and Veggie-Ham Potato Patty-Cakes (recipe page 97).

Serves: 6 or 4 with leftovers

Grilled Shrimp Po' Boys

New Orleans Poor Boy sandwiches are served either undressed (plain) or dressed (with condiments). This grilled version of the generally fried classic is dressed "to the nines," slathered with a tangy mustard-horseradish-chive sour cream–mayonnaise sauce and topped with thinly sliced tomatoes and fresh arugula leaves.

⅓ cup mayonnaise

⅓ cup sour cream

1 tablespoon Dijon mustard

1 tablespoon prepared horseradish

1 tablespoon snipped fresh chives

6 ounces leftover Barbecued Jumbo Shrimp (approximately 10 to 12 shrimp)

2 sesame seed buns

1 small tomato, thinly sliced

½ cup packed arugula leaves

Whisk together mayonnaise, sour cream, mustard, horseradish, and chives in a medium bowl. Set aside until needed. Cut shrimp in half horizontally through the body. Place shrimp in a microwave-safe bowl and reheat for 1 minute.

For each sandwich: Cut bun in half horizontally and toast lightly. Spread 1 tablespoon mayonnaise mixture on cut sides of toasted bun. Place half the shrimp on bottom half of bun. Layer half the sliced tomatoes and 5 or 6 arugula leaves atop shrimp. Top with other half of bun. Cut sandwiches in half and serve immediately.

You can substitute baby lettuce leaves for the arugula, but the herb adds a distinctive peppery, mustardy flavor to this sandwich. (Most supermarkets now offer fresh arugula in their produce sections.) You'll have extra mayonnaise mixture left over for use in other sandwiches. Try it with ham, turkey, or roast beef. Refrigerate mayonnaise in a covered container for up to 1 week.

Serves: 2

Caribbean Shrimp Wraps

Known as the Mexican potato, jicama is a brown-skinned root vegetable that tastes like a cross between a raw white potato and a cucumber. Most often peeled and eaten raw, jicama is crunchy with a sweet, nutty flavor.

¼ cup creamy peanut butter

1 teaspoon gingerroot paste or grated gingerroot

1 teaspoon garlic paste or finely minced garlic

1 tablespoon honey

2 tablespoons rice vinegar

1 tablespoon soy sauce

1 tablespoon water

Dash cayenne pepper

1 cup leftover Coconut Jasmine Sticky Rice (recipe page 84) or other cooked white rice

¼ cup mango chutney

6 ounces leftover Barbecued Jumbo Shrimp (approximately 10 to 12 shrimp)

4 Mission brand Spinach-Herb Wraps

1 cup julienne-cut carrots

1 cup julienne-cut jicama or cucumber

1 cup quartered red grapes

2 tablespoons chopped peanuts

1 packed cup baby spinach leaves

At least 30 minutes ahead: Whisk together peanut butter, gingerroot, garlic, honey, rice vinegar, soy sauce, water, and pepper in a medium bowl. Set aside until needed.

Mix rice and mango chutney together in a medium bowl. Set aside until needed.

Cut shrimp in half horizontally through the body. Cut each section in half, lengthwise. Set aside until needed.

Working with 1 wrap at a time: Place wrap on clean counter. Spread 1 tablespoon peanut sauce evenly on surface of wrap. Spread 2 tablespoons rice mixture across bottom half of wrap. Place ¼ cup shrimp (about 10 pieces) atop rice in bottom half of wrap. Sprinkle with ¼ cup carrots, ¼ cup jicama, ¼ cup grapes, and ½ tablespoon peanuts. Place about 10 spinach leaves randomly atop entire wrap.

Fold in sides and roll tightly, folding in sides as you roll. Place wrap on a large piece of plastic wrap and roll up tightly. Repeat process with remaining wraps. Refrigerate for at least 30 minutes.

To serve: Remove plastic wrap and microwave for 30 seconds before serving. Cut each wrap in half on a slight diagonal.

You may end up with leftover bits of carrot, jicama, grapes, peanuts, and peanut sauce. Fashion a leftover-makeover-makeover by creating a Caribbean veggie wrap with the remaining ingredients. You can substitute baby lettuce greens for the spinach, bite-sized pieces of grilled chicken for the shrimp, cucumber for the jicama, and apples for the grapes for a different taste treat.

Serves: 4

You Peel 'Em Shrimp with Three Dipping Sauces

You'll have to work for your supper, peeling your own shrimp. But the triple treat of Capered White Sauce, Classic Cocktail Sauce, and Asian Sweet Vinegar Sauce will reward you for your efforts. Serve the shrimp with freshly baked crusty bread and a large tossed salad.

You Peel 'Em Shrimp

24 ounces beer of choice

1½ cups water

1 tablespoon salt

½ cup chopped sweet onions, like Vidalia

¼ teaspoon garlic powder

½ teaspoon celery seeds

1 bay leaf

2 pounds medium easy-peel frozen shrimp (51/60s), thawed

Place beer, water, salt, onions, garlic powder, celery seeds, and bay leaf in a large pot over high heat. Bring to a boil, add shrimp, and reduce heat to medium. Boil shrimp until pink, about 2 to 3 minutes (do not overcook.) Drain in a colander. Discard bay leaf.

To serve: Place shrimp in a large serving bowl. Divide each of the 3 sauces (opposite) among 6 individual dipping-sauce dishes and serve immediately with lots of napkins.

Easy-peel shrimp are shrimp in the shell that have been deveined before they were frozen. You can substitute larger shrimp if you like and if your budget allows, but I have found that the smaller frozen shrimp are more often on sale. My supermarket occasionally runs a "Buy one bag, get two bags free" sale, so I stock up.

Serves: 6 or 4 with leftovers

CAPERED WHITE SAUCE

6 tablespoons mayonnaise

1 teaspoon Dijon mustard

1 tablespoon finely minced shallots

½ tablespoon rinsed and drained capers

½ teaspoon dried basil

½ teaspoon dried tarragon

Freshly ground black pepper

Up to 2 days ahead: Mix together mayonnaise, mustard, shallots, capers, basil, tarragon, and black pepper to taste in a small bowl. Cover and refrigerate until needed. (Makes ½ cup.)

....

CLASSIC COCKTAIL SAUCE

6 tablespoons ketchup

1 tablespoon prepared horseradish

½ tablespoon fresh lime juice

¼ teaspoon celery seeds

¼ teaspoon Worcestershire sauce

Hot sauce

Up to 2 days ahead: Mix together ketchup, horseradish, lime juice, celery seeds, Worcestershire sauce, and 2 healthy dashes hot sauce in a small bowl. Cover and refrigerate until needed. (Makes ½ cup.)

....

ASIAN SWEET VINEGAR SAUCE

3 tablespoons rice vinegar

2 tablespoons soy sauce

1 tablespoon ketchup

1 tablespoon brown sugar

2 tablespoons toasted sesame oil

¼ teaspoon cornstarch

½ teaspoon water

Up to 2 days ahead: Mix together vinegar, soy sauce, ketchup, brown sugar, and sesame oil in a small nonstick saucepan over medium heat until boiling. Mix cornstarch with water in a small bowl. Stir into vinegar mixture and cook until sauce has thickened, about 2 minutes. Transfer to a small covered container and refrigerate until needed. (Makes ½ cup.)

....

Shrimp Risotto

Arborio rice is an Italian white, oval, short-grain rice that has a high starch content. Cooking releases the starch, giving the rice a creamy, chewy consistency that absorbs flavors well. Arborio rice in a good risotto should be cooked al dente.

1½ cups seafood broth

3 cups water

3 tablespoons butter

½ cup chopped sweet onions, like Vidalia

2 teaspoons garlic paste or finely minced garlic

1 tablespoon tomato paste

1½ cups arborio rice

1 cup white wine

2 cups seeded, diced plum tomatoes

3 tablespoons snipped fresh flat-leaf parsley

½ pound leftover cooked and peeled You Peel 'Em Shrimp, cut in half horizontally

2 tablespoons grated Parmesan cheese

Place broth and water in a medium saucepan over medium heat and bring to a boil. Reduce heat to low and allow broth to simmer.

Melt butter in a large nonstick saucepan over medium heat. Add onions and sauté until soft, about 1 minute. Add garlic and tomato paste and sauté, stirring frequently, for 1 minute. Add rice and cook, stirring frequently, for 1 minute. Add wine and cook until liquid is absorbed, stirring frequently.

Add ½ cup warm broth to rice. Stir constantly, until liquid is absorbed. Continue adding broth mixture ½ cup at a time (reserving final ½ cup broth for final step), stirring constantly, until rice is tender but firm to the bite. (Taste a few grains of rice after each ½ cup of broth is absorbed.) Stir in tomatoes, parsley, shrimp, and final ½ cup broth, and cook until liquid has been absorbed and mixture is creamy. Stir in Parmesan cheese and serve immediately. Top each serving with extra Parmesan cheese if desired.

You'll find seafood broth in the soup section of your supermarket. Or make your own shrimp broth and freeze it: Use the shells left from peeling shrimp for the Barbecued Jumbo Shrimp recipe (page 70). Place shells and 1 quart water in a large soup pot over medium-high heat. Add 2 sticks celery, halved; 1 medium carrot, cut in thirds; 1 medium peeled onion, quartered; 2 cups cream sherry; 6 ounces tomato juice; ½ teaspoon cayenne pepper; and ½ teaspoon white pepper. Bring to boil, reduce heat to low, and cover pot. Simmer broth for 2 hours. Strain broth through a sieve into a large bowl. Transfer broth to 1½-cup covered containers and freeze until needed.

Serves: 4

Savory Shrimp Tart

You can assemble and bake this tart up to an hour ahead of time. Allow it to rest at room temperature, then reheat it in a 300°F oven for 10 minutes. The tart tastes great served at room temperature as well.

2 tablespoons olive oil

1 large sweet onion, like Vidalia, cut in half and thinly sliced

2 teaspoons garlic paste or finely minced garlic

½ cup snipped fresh basil plus 4 whole leaves

1 9-inch rolled, refrigerated Pillsbury Ready Crust

3 ounces leftover You Peel 'Em Shrimp, peeled and cut in half horizontally

6 ounces (3 large) plum tomatoes, sliced ¼ inch thick and drained on paper toweling

½ teaspoon coarse salt

½ teaspoon cracked pepper

1 cup shredded Gruyère cheese

1 egg yolk

1 teaspoon heavy cream or milk

Preheat oven to 375°F. Place olive oil in a large nonstick skillet over medium heat. Add onions and sauté, stirring frequently, until browned and caramelized, about 7 minutes. Reduce heat to medium-low. Add garlic and ½ cup snipped basil and sauté, stirring constantly, for 30 seconds. Remove from heat and transfer onion mixture to a medium bowl. Allow onions to cool.

Allow pie crust to reach room temperature. Unroll pie crust onto a large sheet of parchment paper. Using a rolling pin, roll pie crust to an 11-inch diameter. Lift edges of parchment paper and invert crust into a 10-inch fluted tart pan with a loose bottom. Press crust into bottom and into flutes, draping excess 1 inch over sides of pan. Spread cooled onion mixture in the bottom of the crust. Place shrimp in an even layer atop onions. Place tomatoes in an even layer atop shrimp. Season tomatoes with salt and pepper. Sprinkle cheese over tomatoes.

Fold excess pie crust inward over tart. Whisk egg yolk and cream together in a small bowl. Brush mixture over the folded crust. Bake tart for 25 to 35 minutes, until crust has browned, cheese has melted, and tart is bubbly. Cool on a wire rack for 10 minutes. Stack whole basil leaves and roll them into a tight pencil-like tube. Snip basil into a chiffonade with kitchen scissors. Sprinkle basil over tart. Push up on bottom of tart pan, removing tart from its fluted perimeter. Cut into serving pieces and serve immediately.

A chiffonade is very thin strips of large-leafed herbs and green-leafed vegetables.

Serves: 6

Herbed Shrimp Cakes

Serve shrimp cakes over a tossed salad with Peach Vinaigrette Drizzle (recipe page 39). Or place them in toasted buns topped with Horseradish Cream Sauce (recipe page 33). For something really different, place a shrimp cake atop a toasted English muffin and top with a poached egg and hollandaise sauce to create Shrimp Benedict.

1 strip bacon, cut into thin pieces

1 tablespoon finely minced shallots

⅓ cup finely diced red or orange bell peppers

⅓ cup finely diced celery

½ teaspoon garlic paste or finely minced garlic

8 ounces leftover You Peel 'Em Shrimp, peeled, cut in half lengthwise, and thinly sliced

1 tablespoon snipped fresh flat-leaf parsley

1 tablespoon snipped fresh cilantro

1 tablespoon snipped fresh basil

¼ cup fresh bread crumbs

½ teaspoon seafood seasoning

Pinch cayenne pepper

1 egg

1 tablespoon heavy whipping cream or milk

1½ tablespoons canola oil

1½ tablespoons butter

One hour ahead: Place bacon in a medium nonstick skillet over medium heat. Fry bacon for 1 minute. Add shallots and sauté, stirring frequently, for 1 minute. Add bell peppers, celery, and garlic, sautéing for 1 minute more. Transfer to a large mixing bowl and allow mixture to cool.

Add shrimp, parsley, cilantro, basil, bread crumbs, seafood seasoning, and pepper to bacon mixture, and toss to combine. Whisk egg and cream together in a small bowl. Add to shrimp mixture and stir until bread crumbs are well moistened.

Place an 8-inch piece of plastic wrap on kitchen counter. Pack shrimp mixture into a ½-cup measure. Up-end mixture onto plastic wrap. Flatten into a tight patty with a firm spatula. Fold plastic wrap securely over shrimp cake. Refrigerate for 1 hour. Repeat this process 3 more times with remaining shrimp mixture.

To cook: Place oil and butter in a large nonstick skillet over medium heat. Unwrap shrimp cakes. When butter has melted, transfer shrimp cakes to skillet with a firm spatula. Fry cakes for 2 minutes per side, until crusty and golden. Serve immediately.

Because this recipe contains little bread crumb filler, the shrimp-packed cakes hold together fragilely. Use a firm spatula and a gentle touch when turning the cakes over.

Serves: 4

Supporting Players
Rounding Out the Meal

Tomato-Spinach Orzo
- Pork Tenderloin–Orzo Soup

Dirty Rice Pilaf
- Vegetable Pilaf Pizza

Coconut Jasmine Sticky Rice
- Jasmine Rice Croquettes

Basmati Rice Stuffed Tomatoes
- Tomato-Rice Soup

Wild and Brown Cranberry Rice
- Chicken-Cashew-Rice Baked Pineapple

Potato, Onion, and Bacon Bake
- Spanish Omelette

Cheesy Hash Browns
- "Everything and the Kitchen Sink" Dinner Pie

Salt-crusted Baked New Potatoes
- Vinaigrette Potato Salad

Mashed Potato Gratin
- Veggie-Ham-Potato Patty-Cakes

Baby Asparagus with Orange-Chive-Mustard Sauce
- Ham and Orange-Chive-Mustard Asparagus Pie

Candied Carrots
- Coconut-Almond Carrot Soup

Spaghetti Squash Primavera
- Spaghetti Squash–Sausage Pie

Roasted Butternut Squash-Sweet Potato–Pesto Mash
- Butternut-Pear-Sweet Potato Soup

Tomato-Spinach Orzo

This orzo is great served with Grilled Peachy Pork Tenderloin (recipe page 38). You can use leftovers from the pork and the orzo to create an easy, tasty soup (recipe follows).

1½ cups dried orzo

½ cup minced red onions

1½ cups chiffonade-snipped fresh baby spinach

¼ cup pine nuts, toasted

¼ cup snipped fresh basil

1½ cups seeded, diced (½-inch) tomatoes

1 cup diced (½-inch) fresh mozzarella (about 4 slices or 4 ounces)

2 tablespoons rice vinegar

2 tablespoons extra-virgin olive oil

1 teaspoon salt

¾ teaspoon freshly ground black pepper

Bring a large saucepan of water to boil over high heat. Add orzo, reduce heat to medium-high, and cook to manufacturer's instructions until al dente, about 10 to 12 minutes.

Meanwhile, place onions, spinach, pine nuts, basil, tomatoes, and mozzarella in a large bowl. Whisk together vinegar, olive oil, salt, and pepper in a small bowl.

Drain orzo in a colander and add to vegetable mixture. Toss to combine. Drizzle vinaigrette over orzo mixture and toss until ingredients are well coated. Serve immediately.

You can substitute white balsamic vinegar for rice vinegar, feta cheese for mozzarella, fresh snipped dill for basil, or toasted sliced almonds for pine nuts.

Serves: 10 or 4 with leftovers

Pork Tenderloin–Orzo Soup

Orzo — the Italian word for barley — is actually pasta that resembles grains of barley or rice. It absorbs flavors well, so orzo is the perfect addition to soups of all kinds.

2 tablespoons olive oil

1 cup chopped sweet onions, like Vidalia

2 teaspoons garlic paste or minced garlic

½ teaspoon crushed red pepper flakes

½ cup minced celery

½ cup minced baby carrots

2 tablespoons tomato paste

6 cups vegetable broth (3 large bouillon cubes/6 cups boiling water)

4 to 5 cups leftover Tomato-Spinach Orzo

1 cup minced leftover Grilled Peachy Pork Tenderloin (recipe page 38)

Heat olive oil in a large saucepan over medium-high heat. Add onions, garlic, red pepper flakes, celery, and carrots. Sauté for 5 minutes, until vegetables have softened slightly. Stir in tomato paste. Cook for 2 minutes longer, stirring frequently. Add vegetable bouillon and stir to combine. Bring mixture to a boil, reduce heat to low. Add orzo and simmer, uncovered, for 10 minutes, stirring occasionally. Add pork and simmer for 5 minutes more. Serve immediately.

Recipe is based on proportions of leftover orzo and pork tenderloin. Adjust amount of bouillon based on how much of these ingredients you are using. Other ingredient amounts can remain the same.

Serves: 6 (1½-cup servings)

Dirty Rice Pilaf

Dirty Rice originated in Louisiana among folks who stretched their nickels by adding chicken livers and gizzards to rice to create an inexpensive main meal. These additions made the rice dark in color. Dirty in name only, this vegetarian version gets its cloudy appearance from the vegetable broth.

1 tablespoon olive oil

1 cup chopped sweet onions, like Vidalia

1½ cups basmati rice, washed and drained

2 tablespoons pine nuts, dry-toasted

2 cups vegetable broth

1 cup water

¼ teaspoon crushed red pepper flakes

½ teaspoon salt

¼ teaspoon allspice

⅓ cup golden raisins

¼ cup chopped dried apricots

1 tablespoon grated lime zest (peel from 1 lime)

2 tablespoons sliced almonds, dry-toasted

Place olive oil in a large nonstick skillet over medium heat. Add onions and sauté until onions have softened, about 3 minutes. Add rice and pine nuts and sauté for 3 more minutes, stirring frequently.

Add broth, water, red pepper flakes, salt, and allspice. Increase heat to high. Bring to a boil, then reduce heat to low. Add raisins, apricots, and lime zest. Cover and simmer until rice is tender and liquid has been absorbed, about 20 minutes.

Fluff rice with a fork, transfer to a serving bowl, and sprinkle with toasted almonds.

You can substitute vegetable bouillon cubes and hot water for vegetable broth. You can use dark raisins instead of golden.

Serves: 8 to 10 or 4 to 6 with leftovers

Vegetable Pilaf Pizza

This veggie-rice pizza is perfect for those who have to avoid wheat and/or gluten. Top with any of your favorite vegetables.

3 cups leftover Dirty Rice Pilaf

2 eggs, beaten

1 (8-ounce) package finely shredded mozzarella cheese (about 3 cups), divided

1 cup bottled marinara sauce

1 cup sliced baby bella or white button mushrooms

½ cup chopped red bell peppers

½ cup chopped green bell peppers

Preheat oven to 400°F. Coat a 12-inch nonstick pizza pan with vegetable cooking spray. Place rice, eggs, and 1 cup mozzarella cheese in a large bowl. Toss until ingredients are well combined. Press mixture evenly in the pizza pan. Bake rice crust for 10 minutes.

Spread marinara sauce over baked crust. Sprinkle with ½ cup mozzarella cheese. Top cheese with mushrooms and bell peppers. Sprinkle remaining mozzarella over vegetables.

Bake for 10 minutes, until cheese is melted and edges of rice crust are crispy. Remove from oven. Cut into 8 slices with a kitchen knife. With a firm spatula, transfer 2 slices to each dinner plate..

This pizza needs to be eaten with a fork, not out of hand.

Serves: 4

Coconut Jasmine Sticky Rice

Often called "Thai fragrant rice," jasmine rice is a long-grained rice with a nutty aroma.
When cooked in coconut milk, the grains stick together, creating a rich, aromatic delicacy.

2 cups jasmine rice, rinsed and drained

2 (13.5-ounce) cans light coconut milk

1½ cups water

2 tablespoons grated lemon peel (2 lemons)

2 teaspoons gingerroot paste or finely minced gingerroot

1 teaspoon garlic paste or finely minced garlic

1 teaspoon salt

Place rice, coconut milk, water, lemon peel, gingerroot, garlic, and salt in a large nonstick saucepan. Bring to a boil, uncovered, over high heat. Reduce heat to low, stir, and cover. Simmer for 20 to 25 minutes, or until the liquid has been absorbed and rice is tender. Fluff rice with a fork.

🙂 You can hold the rice for up to 15 minutes. Place 3 sheets of paper toweling over top of saucepan and replace lid. (This absorbs excess moisture from the steamed rice.) Before serving, reheat on low heat for 1 minute and fluff rice with a fork.

Serves: 8 or 4 to 6 with leftovers

Jasmine Rice Croquettes

Leftover rice takes a star turn as a croquette in this recipe. Combined with fresh herbs and tomatoes, the fried rice cakes make a great crunchy side dish alongside grilled steaks, chops, fish, or chicken.

2 cups leftover Coconut Jasmine Sticky Rice
½ cup chopped sweet onions, like Vidalia
½ cup finely diced grape tomatoes, drained
1 tablespoon snipped fresh flat-leaf parsley
1 tablespoon snipped fresh chives
1 tablespoon snipped fresh thyme
¼ teaspoon salt
⅛ teaspoon ground white pepper
1 egg, beaten
2 tablespoons canola oil

At least 1 hour and up to 3 hours ahead: Mix rice, onions, tomatoes, parsley, chives, thyme, salt, and pepper together in a medium bowl. Add egg and stir until all ingredients are well moistened. With clean hands, form rice into 6 well-packed balls. Flatten each with a firm spatula and pat into a compact patty. Place patties on a plate, cover with plastic wrap, and refrigerate for at least 1 hour.

To fry: Place 1 tablespoon oil in a large nonstick skillet over medium heat. Working in 2 batches: When oil is hot, carefully transfer 3 rice patties to skillet with a firm spatula. Cook for 2 minutes. Carefully turn patties over, using a second spatula if necessary. Cook for 2 minutes more, until croquettes are browned and crispy. Transfer croquettes to a serving plate. Repeat with remaining 3 croquettes. Serve immediately.

The rice and other ingredients hold together very tenuously, so be very careful as you transfer and turn the croquettes. If parts break away, press them back into the patty with your clean fingers or the spatula.

Serves: 6

Basmati Rice Stuffed Tomatoes

The most fragrant of all types of rice, basmati rice is grown in India and Pakistan. The rice needs to be washed until the water runs clear to remove the starch clinging to its grains.

4 large, firm, ripe tomatoes

Salt and freshly ground black pepper

½ cup basmati rice, washed 3 times and drained in a colander

⅓ cup currants

¼ cup pine nuts

1 tablespoon olive oil

1 teaspoon crushed garlic or garlic paste

½ cup chopped sweet onions, like Vidalia

½ teaspoon dried marjoram

2 tablespoons fresh snipped basil

2 tablespoons grated Parmesan cheese

Up to 1 day ahead: Cut tops off tomatoes and set aside. Scoop pulp from tomatoes with a small spoon and place in a blender. Sprinkle insides of tomatoes with salt and place them upside-down on paper toweling to drain. Chop tomato tops and set aside.

Pulse tomato pulp until pureed. Transfer to a 1-cup liquid measuring cup. Add water if needed to make 1 cup. Place tomato puree, rice, and ¼ teaspoon salt in a medium nonstick saucepan over high heat. When mixture comes to a boil, reduce heat to low, cover saucepan, and cook for 18 to 20 minutes, or until liquid is almost absorbed and rice is barely cooked.

While rice is cooking, soak currants in enough water to cover for 5 minutes. Drain and set aside. Place pine nuts in a small nonstick skillet over medium-low heat. Toast nuts, stirring occasionally, for 3 to 4 minutes, until they just start to brown. Set aside.

Heat olive oil in a large nonstick skillet over medium heat. Add garlic and onions and sauté, stirring frequently, for 3 minutes, or until onions are translucent. Add chopped tomato tops, currants, pine nuts, and marjoram. Stir to combine. Add cooked rice, basil, ¼ teaspoon salt, and freshly ground black pepper to taste. Cook rice mixture for 1 minute, stirring constantly. Remove skillet from heat.

Stuff tomatoes with rice mixture, forming a mound of rice on top. Coat an 8-inch-square baking dish with vegetable cooking spray. Place tomatoes in dish and cover snugly with plastic wrap. Refrigerate until needed.

To bake: Preheat oven to 350°F. Remove plastic wrap and sprinkle tomatoes with Parmesan cheese. Bake tomatoes, uncovered, for 15 minutes, until rice is heated through and tomatoes are still firm. Serve immediately.

Use leftovers from this recipe to make Tomato-Rice Soup. You'll need 2 stuffed tomatoes.

Serves: 4

Tomato-Rice Soup

Making hot soup doesn't get any easier than this. All the flavorings are packed into the rice and tomatoes, so all you need to do is add broth.

2 large chicken bouillon cubes plus 4 cups hot water or 4 cups chicken broth
2 leftover Basmati Rice Stuffed Tomatoes (about 2 cups)

Crumble bouillon cubes in a large saucepan over medium heat. Add 4 cups hot water and stir until bouillon in dissolved.

Remove rice mixture from Stuffed Tomatoes and add it to the chicken broth. Peel, core, and chop tomatoes and add to the broth. Stir ingredients. Reduce heat to low and simmer for 10 minutes. Serve immediately.

For a heartier meal, add bite-size pieces of leftover chicken, beef, pork, ham, shrimp, or meatballs to soup before simmering.

Serves: 6

Wild and Brown Cranberry Rice

You'll find wild rice and brown or white rice mixtures in most large supermarkets or gourmet stores.

1 cup brown and wild rice mixture

1½ tablespoons butter

1 cup finely chopped white button mushrooms

½ cup chopped sweet onions, like Vidalia

⅓ cup finely chopped celery

1 cup sweetened dried cranberries

Up to 4 hours ahead: Wash rice until water runs clear. Drain in a colander. Place rice in a large nonstick saucepan. Add 3 cups water. Bring to a boil over medium heat. Cover and reduce heat to low. Simmer for 35 minutes. Remove cover, fluff rice with a fork, and simmer until all the water has evaporated, about 15 minutes more. Fluff rice with a fork.

Meanwhile, melt butter in a large nonstick skillet over medium heat. Add mushrooms, onions, celery, and cranberries. Sauté, stirring frequently, for 5 minutes, until onions are soft and mushroom liquid has evaporated. Toss vegetables with rice. Serve immediately or transfer to a large serving bowl. Cover bowl with plastic wrap and refrigerate until needed.

To serve: Reheat rice in the microwave for 2 to 3 minutes before serving.

If you can't find a brown and wild rice mixture, substitute a mixture of white and wild rice. The texture will be a little different, but the dish will be equally as tasty.

Serves: 8 or 4 with leftovers

Chicken-Cashew-Rice Baked Pineapple

This spectacular presentation of Thai chicken rice is sure to wow your family or friends. Place each stuffed pineapple half on a serving plate and place it between two diners to share.

1 fresh pineapple

1 tablespoon olive oil

¾ pound boneless chicken breast, cut into ½-inch dice

6 tablespoons fish sauce

2 tablespoons Asian sweet chili sauce

6 tablespoons sugar

½ cup coconut milk

¾ cup whole cashews, cut in half lengthwise

¾ cup raisins

3 tablespoons snipped fresh cilantro

3 cups leftover Wild and Brown Cranberry Rice

1 cup leftover cooked white rice or Dirty Rice Pilaf (recipe page 82)

Up to 2 hours ahead: Cut pineapple in half lengthwise. Cut around the perimeter of the pineapple with a small serrated knife. Cut pineapple out of shell, being careful not to pierce shell. Drain pineapple shell upside-down on paper toweling. Finely chop pineapple and set aside.

Place olive oil in a large skillet over medium heat. Add chicken and sauté, stirring frequently, until just cooked through, 2 to 3 minutes. Add fish sauce, chili sauce, sugar, and coconut milk. Cook, stirring occasionally, until liquid is foamy. Remove skillet from heat.

Stir in ¾ cup chopped pineapple (refrigerate remainder in a covered container), cashews, raisins, cilantro, and rice. Transfer chicken and rice mixture in a large mound to the 2 hollowed-out pineapple shells. Cover pineapples with aluminum foil and refrigerate until needed.

To bake and serve: Preheat oven to 350°F. Remove foil and place stuffed pineapple halves on a large baking sheet. Bake for 20 to 30 minutes, until mixture has heated through and rice has browned slightly.

This is a great recipe to use up any small amounts of leftover rice you may have in your freezer. You can use any combination of leftover rice in this recipe.

Serves: 4

Potato, Onion, and Bacon Bake

Yukon Gold was the first Canadian-grown potato variety to be marketed in the U.S. by name. Other yellow potatoes, equally as good, are now available. They all have a rich golden color and a creamy, buttery flavor.

4 ounces bacon (about 4 slices), thinly sliced crosswise

1½ pounds Yukon Gold potatoes, peeled and thinly sliced

1½ large sweet onions, like Vidalia, halved and thinly sliced

⅓ cup butter, cut into small dice

Salt and freshly ground black pepper

Preheat oven to 400°F. Place bacon pieces in the bottom of an 8-inch-diameter baking dish that is at least 4 inches deep. Cover bacon with one-third of the potatoes, then layer one-third of onions atop the potatoes. Sprinkle one-third of the butter bits over vegetables and season with salt and pepper. Repeat layering and seasoning two more times. Bake, uncovered, for 1 hour, until potatoes are golden brown and top onions are crispy.

Use the leanest bacon you can find. For added flavor, try smoked or maple-flavored bacon.

Serves: 6 or 4 with leftovers

Spanish Omelette

The most famous tapa in Spain, tortilla de patatas *is a dish that traditionally combines an egg omelette with fried potatoes. It makes a great brunch or a quick, easy supper entrée.*

2 cups leftover Potato, Onion, and Bacon Bake

¼ cup slivered roasted red peppers (from a jar)

4 eggs, beaten

¼ teaspoon black pepper

½ cup shredded Swiss cheese

Coat a large nonstick skillet with vegetable cooking spray. Place over medium heat. Spread leftover Potato, Onion, and Bacon Bake in the bottom of skillet. Cook for 5 minutes, until bacon is sizzling and potatoes have warmed through. Sprinkle roasted red peppers over potatoes. Whisk eggs and pepper together in a small bowl. Pour eggs evenly over potatoes and cook for 6 to 8 minutes, pulling the sides of the omelette away from the edges of skillet with a spatula and tipping the still-liquid eggs from the top to the sides.

When the omelette is nearly set, with just a little liquid egg on top, place a dinner plate atop skillet and flip omelette onto plate. Slide flipped omelette back into skillet and cook 5 minutes more. Sprinkle omelette with cheese, cover, and cook for 2 more minutes or just until cheese has started to melt.

Cut omelette into 4 wedges and serve immediately.

Substitute any shredded cheese of your choice. The recipe is based on 2 cups leftover Potato, Onion, and Bacon Bake. Adjust amounts of other ingredients according to how many cups of the leftovers you are using.

Serves: 4

Cheesy Hash Browns

These yummy potatoes take 1½ hours to bake, so plan your timing ahead.

1 (30-ounce) package frozen country-style hash brown potatoes, thawed

1 cup peeled, cored, and chopped sweet-tart apples, like Empire (1 large apple)

1 cup chopped sweet onions, like Vidalia

2 tablespoons snipped fresh chives

½ teaspoon salt

½ teaspoon black pepper

2 cups shredded sharp cheddar cheese

1 (10.75-ounce) can cream of chicken soup

1 cup sour cream

1½ tablespoons dried onion flakes

1 cup fresh bread crumbs

¼ cup butter, melted

Early in the day or 1 day ahead: Pat potatoes dry with paper toweling. Place potatoes in a large bowl. Add apples, onions, chives, salt, and pepper, and toss to combine.

Coat a 9x13-inch baking dish with vegetable cooking spray. Spread potato mixture in an even layer in the dish. Place shredded cheese, chicken soup, sour cream, and onion flakes in a medium bowl. Stir to mix ingredients well. Drop cheese mixture by spoonfuls over potatoes, then spread over potatoes. Cover with plastic wrap and refrigerate until needed.

To bake: Preheat oven to 350°F. Bake potatoes, uncovered, for 1 hour. Remove baking dish from oven and sprinkle bread crumbs over potato mixture. Drizzle crumbs with ¼ cup melted butter. Return potatoes to oven and bake for 30 minutes more, until crumbs are browned and crunchy.

You can substitute any of your favorite sweet-tart apples in this recipe. The dried onion flakes, however, are essential. Raw onions don't give the dish enough of an onion flavor.

Serves: 8 to 10 or 4 to 6 with leftovers

"Everything and the Kitchen Sink" Dinner Pie

This savory dinner pie is a great way to use up all kinds of leftovers littering your refrigerator or freezer. You are limited only by your imagination.

Half the leftover Cheesy Hash Browns (about 3 cups)
1 cup diced Orange-Mustard Glazed Baked Ham (recipe page 33) or other ham
1½ cups diced leftover vegetables (such as asparagus, mushrooms, spinach)
1 cup shredded sharp cheddar cheese
6 large eggs
½ cup heavy whipping cream
4 dashes hot sauce or Tabasco sauce
Salt and black pepper to taste
½ cup sliced large cherry tomatoes or plum tomatoes
2 tablespoons grated Parmesan cheese
Sour cream

Preheat oven to 400°F. Coat a deep-dish pie plate with vegetable cooking spray. Press hash browns into bottom and along sides of pie plate to form a thick crust. Sprinkle ham over bottom of crust. Sprinkle vegetables and shredded cheese over ham.

Whisk eggs, cream, hot sauce, salt, and pepper together in a medium bowl. Pour egg mixture over ham, vegetables, and cheese. Press tomatoes into egg mixture. Sprinkle Parmesan cheese over tomatoes.

Bake, uncovered for 35 to 50 minutes, until a knife inserted in the center of the pie comes out clean. (If top starts to get too brown before egg mixture has set, cover with aluminum foil.) Serve each portion with a dollop of sour cream.

You can use 1½ cups of any of your favorite vegetables in this recipe, and you can substitute leftover chicken, shrimp, Italian sausage, beef, or pork for the ham. Freeze leftover scraps from multiple meals and use them in this dish, keeping the proportions the same.

Serves: 6 to 8

Salt-crusted Baked New Potatoes

This recipe will feed a crowd. The proportions are designed so that you'll have enough potatoes left over to make potato salad the next day. Cut the ingredients in half if you don't plan on making the salad.

4 pounds small red new potatoes

¼ cup olive oil

2 teaspoons cracked pepper

2 teaspoons coarse salt

Preheat oven to 350°F. Place potatoes, oil, pepper, and salt in a large bowl. Toss until potatoes are well coated with other ingredients. Transfer potatoes to a large shallow baking dish. Bake potatoes for 45 minutes or until tender when poked with a fork. Serve immediately.

You can use small white potatoes or fingerling potatoes in this recipe. The coarse (kosher) salt and cracked pepper are essential.

Serves: 10 to 12 or 6 to 8 with leftovers

Vinaigrette Potato Salad

Made without mayonnaise, this easy potato salad can be served warm, cold, or at room temperature. You can prepare it up to one day ahead.

2 pounds leftover Salt-crusted Baked New Potatoes

2 tablespoons white balsamic or white wine vinegar

1 teaspoon sugar

3 tablespoons finely minced shallots

1 tablespoon stone-ground mustard

1 tablespoon canola oil

3 tablespoons snipped curly parsley

At least 3 hours or up to 1 day ahead: Cut potatoes into ½-inch-thick slices. Place in a large bowl. Set aside.

Whisk vinegar, sugar, shallots, and mustard together in a small bowl. Whisk in the oil. Pour vinaigrette over potatoes and toss to combine. Add parsley and toss with potatoes. Transfer to a covered container and refrigerate so that flavors marry. Serve cold or transfer to a serving bowl and microwave for 2 minutes or until heated through.

You can substitute chopped onions for the shallots, but increase amount to ¼ cup. You can substitute any coarse-grained mustard for the stone-ground.

Serves: 4

Mashed Potato Gratin

The French word "le gratin" was once used in reference to the upper crust of Parisian society. In culinary circles, however, it usually refers to a browned crust of cheese atop a baked dish of potatoes, meat, or vegetables. You'll find no class warfare in this recipe ,because copious amounts of cheese are well mixed with the potatoes.

3 pounds Yukon Gold potatoes, peeled and cut into 2-inch chunks

3½ tablespoons butter

1 (8-ounce) package chive and onion cream cheese, softened at room temperature

2 eggs, beaten

1 cup milk

1 cup shredded Gruyère cheese

½ teaspoon salt

¼ teaspoon black pepper

Up to 1 day ahead: Place potatoes in a large saucepan with water to cover. Boil over medium heat until cooked through, about 15 to 18 minutes. Drain in a colander.

Put potatoes through a ricer or place in a bowl and mash with a potato masher. Stir in 3 tablespoons butter, cream cheese, eggs, milk, and shredded cheese. Season with salt and pepper.

Grease a large casserole dish with ½ tablespoon butter. Transfer potato mixture to dish. Cover with plastic wrap and refrigerate until needed.

To bake: Preheat oven to 375°F. Bring potatoes to room temperature before baking. Bake, covered with aluminum foil, for 45 minutes. Uncover and bake for 15 minutes more, until potatoes are heated through and the top is golden.

You can substitute herb and garlic cream cheese for the chive and onion and use Fontina or Emmenthaler cheese instead of the Gruyère.

Serves: 8 to 10 or 4 to 6 with leftovers

Veggie-Ham-Potato Patty-Cakes

Patty-cakes aren't just for the baker's man anymore. Enjoy these savory potato cakes as a side dish for dinner, with eggs for breakfast or brunch, or as a quick, nutritious lunch.

1 cup leftover Mashed Potato Gratin

2 tablespoons chopped sweet onions, like Vidalia

1 cup roughly grated zucchini

½ cup roughly grated carrots

½ cup (¼-inch-dice) leftover Orange-Mustard Glazed Baked Ham (recipe page 33)

Freshly ground black pepper

1 tablespoon margarine or clarified butter

At least I hour or up to I month ahead: Place mashed potatoes in a medium microwave-safe bowl and reheat for I minute to soften potatoes. Add onions, zucchini, and carrots to potatoes, and mix together with a large spoon until creamy and well combined. Stir in ham. Working with I patty-cake at a time, place ½ cup potato mixture on a cutting board. Flatten into a 4-inch patty with a firm spatula. Season with pepper to taste.

Transfer patty-cakes to a waxed-paper-lined plate, cover with plastic wrap, and refrigerate, or place each patty-cake on a piece of plastic wrap and fold in all edges to cover. Place wrapped patty-cakes in a freezer-weight zipper bag and freeze until needed. (Remove from plastic wrap and place patty-cakes on a waxed-paper-lined plate, covered with plastic wrap, in the refrigerator to defrost.)

To serve: Melt margarine or clarified butter in a large nonstick skillet over medium-low heat. Add potato-patty-cakes and sauté for I½ minutes. Turn patty-cakes over with a firm spatula. Sauté for I½ minutes. Serve immediately.

 Clarified butter can be used at higher temperatures than regular butter without burning. To make clarified butter, cut a stick of butter into pieces and melt it slowly in a small nonstick saucepan over low heat. The milk solids will sink to the bottom of the pan and froth will form on top. Skim the froth from surface with a spoon. Pour off the clear melted butter into a covered container, discarding the milk solids remaining at the bottom of the saucepan. Store clarified butter in refrigerator up to 4 weeks.

Serves: 4

Baby Asparagus with Orange-Chive-Mustard Sauce

This recipe can be made several hours in advance and served at room temperature, perfect for a large buffet gathering.

½ cup mayonnaise

½ cup sour cream

1 tablespoon snipped fresh chives

2 teaspoons grated orange peel

1 tablespoon fresh orange juice

½ teaspoon Dijon mustard

⅛ teaspoon salt

⅛ teaspoon black pepper

2 pounds thin asparagus, washed and brittle ends snapped off

Olive oil spray

1 tablespoon citrus grill (Durkee), lemon-dill, or lemon pepper seasoning

At least 2 hours or up to 1 day ahead: Mix together mayonnaise, sour cream, chives, orange peel, orange juice, mustard, salt, and pepper in a medium bowl. Transfer to a covered container and refrigerate until needed.

Two hours ahead: Place asparagus in a large skillet with water to cover. Place over medium-high heat and cook until crisp-tender, about 2 minutes. (Watch process carefully and test repeatedly with a fork. Thin asparagus can overcook quickly.)

Drain asparagus in a colander. Rinse with cold water and drain again. Pat dry with paper toweling. Coat asparagus with olive oil spray. Sprinkle seasoning over asparagus, tossing with clean hands until asparagus is well coated. Transfer to a large serving platter. Cover with plastic wrap and refrigerate until needed.

To serve: Remove plastic wrap from asparagus. Transfer Orange-Chive-Mustard Sauce to a glass bowl. Place bowl on platter with asparagus. Serve cold or at room temperature.

Be sure to stand guard at the stove while cooking the asparagus. It is essential that the vegetable be crisp-tender to retain its deep green color.

Serves: 12 or 8 with leftovers

Ham and Orange-Chive-Mustard Asparagus Pie

Flavorful and custardlike, this easy brunch or dinner pie utilizes leftovers from several recipes featured in this book. You can substitute another meat, seafood, or vegetable, but the Orange-Chive-Mustard Sauce is crucial.

½ tablespoon flour

1 rolled, refrigerated Pillsbury pie crust

½ teaspoon canola oil

½ cup chopped sweet onions, like Vidalia

½ cup leftover Orange-Chive-Mustard Sauce (recipe page 98)

½ cup heavy whipping cream

3 large eggs, beaten

Freshly ground black pepper

⅓ cup grated Gruyère, Swiss, or other strong-flavored cheese

1½ cups shredded 4-Cheese Mexican blend

2 cups (½-inch-dice) leftover Baby Asparagus

1 heaping cup (½-inch-dice) leftover Orange-Mustard Glazed Baked Ham (recipe page 33)

Preheat oven to 375°F. Sprinkle flour on clean counter. Place pie crust on counter and roll out to 10-inch diameter. Place crust in a deep-dish pie plate. Crimp edges and prick several holes in the bottom with a fork. Bake for 7 minutes. Remove from oven and allow crust to cool.

Meanwhile, place canola oil in a small nonstick skillet over medium heat. Add onions and sauté for 1 minute, stirring constantly. Remove from burner and set aside.

Whisk together Orange-Chive-Mustard Sauce, heavy cream, eggs, and black pepper to taste in a medium bowl. When crust is cool, sprinkle half the Gruyère and half the Mexican cheese in the bottom of the crust. Spread onions, asparagus, and ham in the crust. Sprinkle remaining cheeses atop filling. Pour egg mixture over cheese.

Place a 2-inch aluminum foil collar around edges of crust so that it doesn't overcook. Bake for 35 minutes. Remove foil collar and bake for 5 minutes more, until edges are golden and pie has set in the middle. Remove pie to a wire rack and cool for 10 to 15 minutes before slicing.

Rolled Pillsbury pie crusts are found in the refrigerated section of your supermarket (2 in each box). They freeze very well. Defrost to room temperature before using. To make this pie ahead, reduce initial baking time to 30 minutes. Refrigerate, covered, until needed, up to 1 day. Reheat at 350°F for 20 to 25 minutes, until heated through. Fasten an aluminum foil collar around edges of crust for all except the last 5 minutes of baking.

Serves: 8

Candied Carrots

Petite baby carrots are the tiniest carrots now on the market — no bigger than your pinky finger and very sweet. If you use baby carrots instead of the smaller version, cut them in half.

4 cups petite baby carrots
⅓ cup butter
⅓ cup jellied cranberry sauce
¼ cup brown sugar
Salt and freshly ground black pepper

Place carrots in a large saucepan with water to cover. Bring water to a boil and cook over medium heat until carrots are crisp-tender, about 3 minutes. (Test carrots frequently with a fork.) Drain carrots in a colander. Rinse with cold water and drain again.

Meanwhile, place butter, cranberry sauce, and brown sugar in a small nonstick saucepan over low heat. Cook, stirring frequently, until all ingredients have melted and are well blended, about 2 to 3 minutes.

Place drained carrots back in saucepan over low heat. Pour butter sauce over carrots and toss until they are well coated. Serve immediately.

You can cook the carrots ahead of time and refrigerate them until needed. Reheat in the microwave. Don't make the sauce ahead of time because the butter and sugar separates during refrigeration and don't blend well together upon reheating.

Serves: 8 with leftovers

Coconut-Almond Carrot Soup

This exotic little soup is a great way to get extra beta-carotene into your diet and use up leftover Candied Carrots. You can use plain cooked carrots in this soup, but add brown sugar (to taste) to sweeten it up.

1 tablespoon butter

1 teaspoon gingerroot paste or
    finely minced gingerroot

½ teaspoon garlic paste or
    finely minced garlic

2 tablespoons finely minced shallots

1 teaspoon finely minced jalapeño pepper

¼ cup finely diced celery

3 cups chicken broth

½ teaspoon ground cumin

½ teaspoon ground coriander

¼ teaspoon paprika

¼ teaspoon salt

⅛ teaspoon black pepper

2 cups leftover Candied Carrots

1 cup unsweetened coconut milk

¼ cup sliced almonds, dry-toasted

½ tablespoon fresh lime juice

Sour cream

1 tablespoon snipped fresh cilantro

Melt butter in a large soup pot over medium heat. Add gingerroot, garlic, shallots, jalapeños and celery. Sauté 1 minute, stirring constantly. Add broth, cumin, coriander, paprika, salt, pepper, and carrots. Bring mixture to a boil (about 4 minutes), stirring occasionally. When mixture reaches a boil, reduce heat to low. Stir in coconut milk and cook for 5 minutes, stirring occasionally. Remove pot from heat and stir in almonds and lime juice.

Transfer soup to a blender and process at high speed until smooth. Pour soup back into soup pot and keep it warm over low heat until serving. Serve each portion with a dollop of sour cream and a sprinkle of fresh cilantro.

I like to use Pacific brand Organic Free Range Chicken Broth. It is about the same price as regular chicken broth, and it has only 70 mg sodium per cup.

Serves: 4

Spaghetti Squash Primavera

Probably the showiest member of the winter squash family, this squash's flesh, when baked, pulls away from the rind like strands of spaghetti. It is low in calories and rich in nutrients.

2 (2-pound) or 1 (4-pound) spaghetti squash, cut in half and seeded

5 tablespoons butter, divided

½ sweet onion, like Vidalia, thinly sliced (about 1 cup)

1 cup thinly sliced red bell peppers, cut about 1 inch long

1 teaspoon salt

½ teaspoon black pepper

1 cup grated Parmesan cheese, divided

⅓ cup pine nuts, dry-toasted

½ cup snipped fresh flat-leaf parsley

Early in the day: Preheat oven to 350°F. Line a large baking sheet with aluminum foil. Place squash, cut sides down, on foil. Bake for 1 hour, until squash is cooked through and soft to the touch. Remove from oven and cool for 10 minutes. Using a fork, shred squash into a large bowl.

Meanwhile, melt 3 tablespoons butter in a large nonstick skillet over medium heat. Add onions and sauté, stirring frequently, for 2 minutes. Add bell peppers and sauté, stirring frequently, for 3 minutes more. Add remaining 2 tablespoons butter to skillet during the last 1 minute. Add onion mixture to squash and toss to combine well. Season with salt, pepper, and ½ cup Parmesan cheese. Toss to combine. Add pine nuts and parsley and mix well.

Coat a shallow 10-inch-round baking dish with vegetable cooking spray. Transfer squash mixture to baking dish and sprinkle with remaining ½ cup Parmesan cheese. Cover dish with plastic wrap. Refrigerate until needed.

To serve: Preheat oven to 325°F. Bring squash mixture to room temperature. Remove plastic wrap and cover securely with aluminum foil. Bake for 20 minutes, until squash is heated through.

You can heat the squash in the microwave until heated through if you prefer.

Serves: 8 to 10 or 4 to 6 with leftovers.

Spaghetti Squash Sausage Pie

You won't miss the carbs in this gluten-free knockoff of the classic spaghetti pie.

½ pound Jimmy Dean Hot Pork Sausage

2 cups leftover Spaghetti Squash Primavera

1 cup ricotta cheese

1 cup shredded mozzarella cheese

1½ cups tomato and basil marinara sauce

½ cup Parmesan cheese

Early in the day or the day before: Cook sausage in a medium nonstick skillet over medium heat for 4 minutes, breaking up sausage with a wooden spoon until cooked through and crumbly. Remove sausage with a slotted spoon and drain on paper toweling, blotting up excess grease. Set aside.

Coat the bottom and sides of a deep-dish pie plate with vegetable cooking spray. Spread Spaghetti Squash Primavera in an even layer in the bottom of the pie plate. Place sausage in an even layer atop squash. Spread ricotta cheese over sausage. Place shredded mozzarella over ricotta. Top with an even layer of marinara sauce. Sprinkle Parmesan over sauce. Cover with plastic wrap and refrigerate until needed.

To bake: Preheat oven to 350°F. Bake, uncovered, for 30 minutes, until cooked through and bubbly. Allow to rest for 5 minutes before serving.

You can use your favorite hot pork sausage and marinara sauce in this recipe. Serve with crusty bread and a salad.

Serves: 4

Roasted Butternut Squash–Sweet Potato–Pesto Mash

Beige-skinned and vase-shaped, butternut squash is an orange-fleshed winter squash with a sweet, nutty flavor similar to pumpkin.

3 pounds butternut squash, cut in half and seeded

2 large sweet potatoes (about 1 pound)

½ cup mayonnaise

1 egg, beaten

1 tablespoon brown sugar

¼ teaspoon salt

¼ teaspoon black pepper

¼ cup prepared basil pesto

½ cup Japanese panko bread crumbs

¼ cup grated Parmesan cheese

2 tablespoons melted butter

Up to 2 days ahead: Preheat oven to 350°F. Line a large baking sheet with aluminum foil. Place squash, cut side down, on foil. Place sweet potatoes on baking sheet. Bake for 1 hour, until vegetables are baked through and soft. Remove from oven and cool for 10 minutes.

Meanwhile, mix mayonnaise, egg, brown sugar, salt, and pepper together in a small bowl. Scoop squash and sweet potatoes from skins and place in a large bowl. Mash with a spoon until smooth. Pour off any accumulated liquids. Stir in mayonnaise mixture until smooth.

Coat a 2-quart ovenproof serving bowl or baking dish with vegetable cooking spray. Place half the squash mixture in dish. Using a small spoon, dollop 2 tablespoons pesto over squash mixture. Place remaining squash in bowl. Top with dollops of remaining pesto. Use a metal skewer to swirl the pesto through the squash mixture in a decorative fashion.

Mix bread crumbs and Parmesan cheese together in a medium bowl. Pour in melted butter and mix with a fork until crumbs are well coated with butter. Sprinkle buttered crumbs over squash mixture. Cover with plastic wrap and refrigerate until needed.

To bake: Preheat oven to 350°F. Remove plastic wrap from serving bowl and bake, uncovered, for 35 to 45 minutes, until squash is heated through and top is slightly browned.

Use yellow-fleshed sweet potatoes in this recipe. Be sure to drain off as much liquid as possible from the mashed butternut squash and sweet potatoes.

Serves: 8 to 10 or 4 to 6 with leftovers

Butternut-Pear-Sweet Potato Soup

Sprinkle a few chile-lime-flavored tortilla strips atop the soup. The crunch of the chips and the tartness of the lime complement the soup's sweet flavor and smooth texture. Add a tossed salad and some crunchy bread, and you've got dinner.

2 tablespoons butter

1 cup chopped sweet onions, like Vidalia

3 unripe firm Bosc pears, peeled, cored, and chopped

4 cups College Inn White Wine & Herb Chicken Broth
   (or 3 cups chicken broth and ½ cup white wine)

2½ cups orange juice

2 tablespoons honey

4 cups leftover Roasted Butternut Squash–Sweet Potato–Pesto Mash

Salt

Melt butter in a large nonstick soup pot over medium heat. Add onions and sauté for 2 minutes, until soft. Add pears, broth, orange juice, and honey. Bring to a boil over high heat. Reduce heat to low and simmer for 20 minutes, stirring occasionally, until pears are tender.

Add squash mixture and simmer on medium, stirring frequently, until heated through, about 10 minutes. Puree soup in batches in a blender. Return soup to pot over low heat until heated through. Add salt to taste and serve. Or, cool soup and transfer to covered containers and refrigerate or freeze until needed.

You can refrigerate soup for up to 3 days or freeze for up to 1 month. Defrost soup and reheat on low before serving.

Serves: 8 (1½-cup servings)

Clean-Up Crew

Don't Throw It Out!

Breakfast Bread Pudding

Eggnog French Toast

Curried Pumpkin-Mushroom Soup

Greek Egg, Lemon, and Rice Soup

Cranberry Ketchup

Panzanella

Banana-Chocolate Frappe

Pavlova

The Cupboard Is Bare!

Bacon-Egg Rolls

Mango Joes

Pizza for One

Hot Chicken Salad Crescent Rolls

Chile Rellenos

Cheese Grits with Bacon Bits

Sante Fe Vegetable Tortilla Soup

Breakfast Bread Pudding

*What do you do with all that stale nutritious grain bread you were so sure your family would eat? Don't throw it out! This recipe, which can be assembled ahead, makes two batches —
one refrigerated overnight for breakfast the next day and one to be frozen for another meal.*

1 tablespoon butter, divided

8 ounces baby bella mushrooms, sliced

4 cups stale 8-grain bread, cut in ½-inch cubes

2 cups shredded sharp cheddar cheese

10 large eggs

2 cups milk

2 cups half-and-half

1 teaspoon dry mustard

1 teaspoon salt

¼ teaspoon onion powder

⅛ teaspoon black pepper

10 slices bacon, cooked crispy and crumbled

½ cup chopped tomatoes

One day or up to 2 weeks ahead: Melt ½ tablespoon butter in a medium nonstick skillet over medium-low heat. Add mushrooms and sauté, stirring frequently, for 3 minutes. Set aside.

Grease bottom and sides of two aluminum 8x8x1½-inch cake pans with ¼ tablespoon butter each. Arrange 2 cups bread cubes in the bottom of each cake pan. Sprinkle 1 cup cheddar cheese over bread cubes in each pan. Place eggs, milk, half-and-half, dry mustard, salt, onion powder, and pepper in a large bowl. Whisk until well beaten.

Evenly divide egg mixture and pour half over bread cubes in each pan (approximately 3¼ cups per pan). Top each pan with half the crumbled bacon, half the mushrooms, and half the chopped tomatoes. Cover each pan with aluminum foil. Refrigerate one pan overnight. Freeze the other until needed (defrost before baking).

To bake: Preheat oven to 325°F. Bake uncovered for 50 minutes or until a knife inserted in the center comes out clean.

You'll need 2 aluminum foil cake pans (8x8x1½ inches) for this recipe. Served with a fresh green salad, this dish makes a great supper entrée as well. If you want to make this recipe to serve 12, layer ingredients in a 9x13-inch baking dish.

Serves: 12 (each pan serves 6)

Eggnog French Toast

Christmas has come and gone and no one finished off the quart of eggnog you stocked for the holidays. Don't throw it out!

2 cups commercially prepared eggnog

2 large eggs

¼ teaspoon cinnamon

⅛ teaspoon nutmeg

1 loaf (16 ounces) cinnamon swirl bread (12 slices)

1 tablespoon butter or margarine

2 tablespoons confectioners' sugar

Whisk eggnog, eggs, cinnamon, and nutmeg together in a medium bowl. Place 8 slices bread in a 10x13-inch baking dish. Place 4 slices bread in an 8x8-inch baking dish. Pour eggnog mixture over bread in both dishes, so that bread is totally covered and soaks in the liquid.

Place 3 large nonstick skillets or griddle pans over medium heat. Grease each pan with butter. Add soaked bread slices to skillets. Cook bread for 2 minutes or until underside is golden. Turn each slice with a firm spatula. Cook for 1 to 2 minutes more, until undersides are golden. Place confectioners' sugar in a small sieve and sprinkle over French toast. Serve immediately with a side of fresh fruit.

You can eliminate the confectioners' sugar and serve French toast with butter and syrup if you like.

Serves: 6 (2 slices per person)

Curried Pumpkin-Mushroom Soup

That package of button mushrooms has been sitting in the refrigerator a while. You notice some brown spots developing. Don't throw them out! Cut out the brown spots and create a masterpiece. Most of the other ingredients for this dish you'll find in your pantry.

2 tablespoons butter

½ pound button mushrooms, stemmed, wiped clean, and sliced very thin

½ cup chopped sweet onions, like Vidalia

1 teaspoon garlic paste or finely minced garlic

1 teaspoon gingerroot paste or finely minced gingerroot

2 tablespoons flour

2 teaspoons curry powder

3 cups chicken broth

1 (16-ounce) can pumpkin puree

1 (5.5-ounce) can apricot nectar

2 tablespoons honey

1 tablespoon dark brown sugar

1 tablespoon fresh lime juice

½ teaspoon salt

⅛ teaspoon crushed red pepper flakes

⅛ teaspoon ground cumin

Dash nutmeg

1 (14-ounce) can light coconut milk

Melt butter in a large nonstick saucepan over medium-low heat. Add mushrooms, onions, garlic, and gingerroot. Sauté, stirring frequently, until onions are soft and released mushroom liquid has evaporated, about 3 minutes.

Stir flour and curry powder into mushroom mixture. Gradually stir in broth. Bring to a simmer over medium heat. Reduce heat to low. Add pumpkin, apricot nectar, honey, brown sugar, lime juice, salt, red pepper flakes, cumin, and nutmeg. Stir to combine ingredients well. Gradually stir in coconut milk. Simmer on low for 10 minutes before serving.

🍴 Serve soup topped with a dollop of sour cream and a sprinkling of fresh snipped chives or flat-leaf parsley if desired.

Serves: 6

Greek Egg, Lemon, and Rice Soup

This version of the Greek classic, avgolemono, uses up those extra egg yolks and lemons as well as leftover Coconut Jasmine Sticky Rice (recipe page 84).

3 tablespoons butter

1 cup chopped celery

1 cup chopped sweet onions, like Vidalia

¼ teaspoon white pepper

3 tablespoons flour

8 cups chicken broth

6 egg yolks, beaten

½ cup fresh lemon juice

½ teaspoon salt

1½ cup leftover Coconut Jasmine Sticky Rice

Snipped fresh parsley

Melt butter in a large nonstick saucepan over medium heat. Add celery, onions, and pepper and sauté, stirring frequently, until onions are soft, about 2 minutes. Stir in flour, 1 tablespoon at a time. Slowly pour in broth, stirring constantly. Bring to a boil, reduce heat to medium-low, cover saucepan, and cook for 5 minutes, stirring occasionally.

Transfer soup to a blender in 2 batches and puree until smooth. Return soup to saucepan. Allow soup to cool for 5 minutes.

Place egg yolks in a medium bowl. Whisk lemon juice into egg yolks. Slowly pour ¼ cup warm soup into egg and lemon mixture, whisking constantly. Whisk egg and lemon mixture into warm soup. Add salt and rice to soup and stir to combine. Place over low heat until soup is heated through, about 5 minutes, stirring occasionally. Garnish each serving with a sprinkle of fresh parsley.

The addition of jasmine rice in this recipe adds a little bulk to an otherwise delicate-tasting soup. Add leftover chicken or some rotisserie chicken, cut into bite-size pieces, for an even heartier meal.

Serves: 6

Cranberry Ketchup

Thanksgiving has long passed, and you still have a bag of cranberries lurking in the freezer. Don't throw them out! This homemade ketchup tastes great on everything from turkey, ham, and chicken to Fancy Schmancy Meat Loaf (recipe page 54).

1 (12-ounce) bag frozen fresh cranberries, washed and picked through

1 cup white wine vinegar

3 cups chopped sweet onions, like Vidalia

2 teaspoons garlic paste or finely minced garlic

¾ cup sugar

1 tablespoon allspice

1 teaspooon salt

⅔ cup water

Place cranberries, vinegar, onions, garlic, sugar, allspice, salt, and water in a large nonstick saucepan over medium-low heat. Bring to a simmer and cook, stirring frequently, for 20 minutes, until very thick. Remove from heat and cool for 15 minutes.

Transfer cranberry mixture to a blender and puree until smooth. Pour ketchup into glass jars and refrigerate for up to 2 months.

You don't have to defrost the cranberries before cooking, but be sure to carefully pick through them, throwing out any that are shriveled or overripe.

Makes: 2½ cups

Panzanella

Italian cooks waste nothing. Panzanella is a Tuscan bread salad that makes the most out of stale bread and a potpourri of ripe summer garden vegetables. Sunflower seed bread works wonderfully well in this recipe, but you can use any hearty peasant bread. Feel free to improvise, substituting any leftover bits of vegetables from your refrigerator. Just remember to keep the proportions the same.

....

5 ounces stale bread, sliced ½ inch thick and cut into 1-inch pieces (about 3 cups)

1 teaspoon garlic paste or finely minced garlic

2 teaspoons unrinsed capers

2 tablespoons red wine vinegar

¼ teaspoon dry mustard

1 tablespoon sugar

¼ cup extra-virgin olive oil

1½ cups seeded, diced plum tomatoes

1 cup quartered and thinly sliced English cucumber

½ cup quartered and thinly sliced red onions

½ cup thinly sliced orange bell peppers, cut into 1-inch pieces

½ cup (½-inch dice) pepper jack cheese

⅓ cup snipped fresh basil

Salt and freshly ground black pepper

....

One hour ahead: Preheat oven to 400°F. Place bread cubes on a nonstick baking sheet. Bake for 2 minutes. Toss cubes with a spatula. Bake 2 minutes more. Remove from oven and allow them to cool completely.

Meanwhile, whisk together garlic, capers, vinegar, dry mustard, and sugar in a small bowl. Slowly add olive oil, whisking constantly.

Place toasted bread cubes in a large salad bowl. Pour dressing over bread and toss to combine. Add tomatoes, cucumbers, onions, bell peppers, cheese, and basil. Toss until all ingredients are well coated with dressing. Season with salt and black pepper to taste. Cover bowl with plastic wrap and refrigerate for 1 hour so that flavors marry.

....

This salad takes only minutes to toss if you do your prep work early in the day. Toast the bread cubes. Once they cool, place them in a zipper bag and keep them at room temperature until needed. Place dressing in a covered container and put vegetables in small zipper bags. Refrigerate until needed.

Serves: 4 to 6

Banana-Chocolate Frappe

Usually made with ice cream, a frappe is a New England term for what other areas of the United States would call a milk shake. This frappe doesn't need ice cream! Don't throw out those ripe bananas with peels that are turning an unappetizing shade of brown! Peel the bananas, wrap them snugly in plastic wrap, and freeze them until needed for a decadently thick, low-cal shake.

1 frozen banana, cut into 5 pieces

1 cup skim milk

1 teaspoon almond extract

1 tablespoon Ghirardelli Premium Double Chocolate Hot Cocoa mix

Place banana, milk, almond extract, and cocoa mix in a blender. Process on highest speed for 1 minute until frappe is thick and smooth. Serve in a tall glass with a long straw.

You can use any sweetened cocoa mix, but Ghirardelli's is particular rich and flavorful. For a different taste treat, freeze ripe strawberries before they go bad and add them to the frappe as a substitute for the banana or for the cocoa mix.

Serves: 1

Pavlova

These sweet meringue shells — which have a light crispy crust and a soft, sugary interior — will use up your excess egg whites. The dessert, named after Russian ballerina Anna Pavlova, can be served topped with ice cream, sherbet, or sorbet and/or fresh cut-up fruit or berries.

6 large egg whites, at room temperature
1 teaspoon vanilla
½ teaspoon cream of tartar
¼ teaspoon salt
1½ cups sugar

Preheat oven to 275°F. Line 2 large baking sheets with parchment paper. Place egg whites, vanilla, cream of tartar, and salt in the bowl of an electric mixer. Whip on medium speed until soft peaks form, about 3 minutes. Increase speed to medium-high and add sugar, 2 tablespoons at a time, beating about 30 seconds after each addition.

Using a large spoon, make six 4-inch circles of batter, about 1 inch thick, on each parchment-covered baking sheet. Transfer the remaining 1 cup batter to a quart-size zipper bag and seal, pressing out the air. Push on exterior of bag until batter is in the lower corner. Cut corner of bag on the diagonal, forming a pastry bag. Pipe a border rim atop each meringue.

Bake for 1 hour. Turn off oven and allow meringues to completely cool inside the oven, about 2 hours.

The meringues can be stored in an airtight container for up to 2 weeks.

Serves: 12

Bacon-Egg Rolls

White Dollar Rolls can be found at Walmart Superstores, but any 3-inch-diameter dinner roll will work in this recipe. They are a great item to store in your freezer.

4 White Dollar Rolls or other 3-inch-diameter rolls

1 tablespoon butter, melted

¼ cup crispy, cooked, crumbled bacon

3 large eggs

1 teaspoon snipped fresh chives

1 teaspoon snipped fresh cilantro

1 teaspoon snipped fresh basil

1 teaspoon snipped fresh flat-leaf parsley

Salt and freshly ground black pepper

¼ cup shredded Swiss cheese

Preheat oven to 400°F. Cut the top off each roll and set aside. Using a small fork, pull the crumb from each roll, leaving a hollow shell. (If you accidentally break through the outside of the roll, press some crumb back into it.) Brush the inside of each roll with melted butter. Place 1 tablespoon crumbled bacon in the bottom of each roll.

Whisk eggs in a small bowl with herbs and salt and pepper to taste. Pour egg mixture evenly among the 4 hollow bread roll shells.

Place rolls on a baking sheet. Bake for 15 minutes or until eggs are nearly set. Mound 1 tablespoon cheese atop each egg roll. Place roll tops on baking sheet. Bake rolls and tops for 5 minutes. Place tops on egg rolls and serve immediately.

Use 4 teaspoons of any of your favorite fresh herbs. Use leftover diced ham, steak, sausage, or bratwurst in egg rolls. Substitute your favorite shredded cheese.

Serves: 4

Mango Joes

Supper can't get easier — or tastier — than this. If your ground beef is frozen, place it in a freezer-weight zipper bag. Place the bag in a large bowl and cover with tepid water for about 20 minutes. It will only be partially defrosted, but you'll be able to cook it with no problem.

1 teaspoon canola oil

1 to 1⅓ pounds lean ground beef

1 (16-ounce) container fresh mango salsa

½ (6-ounce) can basil, garlic, and oregano tomato paste (about 6 tablespoons)

8 sesame seed buns, cut in half

Preheat oven to 300°F. Place canola oil in a large nonstick skillet over medium heat. Add ground beef and cook, stirring frequently and breaking beef into small pieces, until beef is almost cooked through, about 3 minutes. Add salsa and stir to combine. Stir in tomato paste, reduce heat to low, and cook for 5 more minutes, stirring frequently.

Meanwhile, place cut buns on a baking sheet in the oven until they are lightly toasted. Spoon Mango Joes into toasted buns and serve.

Fresh mango salsa is a great staple to keep on hand. But if you don't have it, use regular fresh or canned tomato salsa and add 1 cup finely chopped fresh or canned fruit, such as peaches or pineapple.

Serves: 8 (½-cup portions)

Pizza for One

This is healthy fast food! Keep naan bread and mozzarella cheese in your freezer and tomato sauce in your pantry and you are all set for a quick pizza on the fly! This is my favorite combination of ingredients, which I usually keep on hand. But if your cupboard is bare, top your pizza with whatever the larder provides.

1 naan bread

2 tablespoons garlic tomato sauce

2 white button mushrooms, sliced

2 tablespoons chopped sweet onions, like Vidalia

½ tomato, thinly sliced

8 thin slices or 1 cup shredded mozzarella cheese

Preheat oven to 425°F. Place naan bread on a nonstick baking sheet. Spread tomato sauce onto bread. Top with mushrooms, onions, tomatoes, and mozzarella. Bake for 7 minutes. Cut into quarters.

Naan, a flatbread commonly eaten in India, Pakistan, and surrounding countries, comes in packages of 3 and keeps for months in the freezer. Much tastier than prepackaged pizza crusts, naan bread comes in a variety of flavors. Most supermarkets now offer them.

Serves: 1

Hot Chicken Salad Crescent Rolls

If you keep these ingredients on hand in your refrigerator and pantry, you'll be able to serve up a savory hot meal in minutes. Serve with a tossed salad.

1 (9.75-ounce) can white chicken breast in water, drained

1 (8-ounce) container whipped cream cheese

2 tablespoons ranch dip mix (½ of a 1-ounce package)

2 tablespoons minced onions

⅓ cup finely minced celery

2 tablespoons finely chopped pecans (optional)

2 (10.1-ounce) packages Pillsbury Big & Buttery Crescent Rolls

Up to 1 week ahead: Mix chicken breast, cream cheese, dip mix, onions, celery, and pecans together in a medium bowl. Transfer to a covered container and refrigerate until needed. (Makes 2 cups.)

Preheat oven to 375°F. Unroll crescent dough and separate at the perforations into 12 large triangles. Place 2 tablespoons chicken salad on the wide end of each triangle. Roll up crescent dough, pressing dough together on each side to seal salad inside the dough. Place on a baking sheet that has been coated with vegetable cooking spray. Bake 15 to 17 minutes, until golden brown. Serve immediately.

You can substitute chopped almonds or peanuts for the pecans. Try experimenting with one of the flavored whipped cream cheeses, like pineapple or chive.

Serves: 6 to 8 (makes 12 rolls)

Chile Rellenos

A quick and easy knockoff of the traditional Mexican cheese-stuffed poblano peppers baked in egg batter, these chile rellenos are made from a few simple ingredients you can keep on hand in your refrigerator or pantry.

2 (4-ounce) cans whole mild green chiles

¼ pound Monterey Jack cheese

2 eggs

¼ cup plus 1 tablespoon milk

1 tablespoon flour

⅛ teaspoon salt

Freshly ground black pepper

1 cup shredded sharp cheddar cheese

Preheat oven to 350°F. Drain chilies in a colander. Cut each pepper lengthwise. Remove any membranes or seeds and rinse with cold water. Open peppers and place them on paper toweling to drain.

Slice Monterey Jack cheese into strips ½x½x1 inch. Fill insides of peppers with cheese strips, folding chiles around cheese. Place, cut-side up, in a 6x9-inch ungreased baking dish.

Whisk together eggs, milk, flour, salt, and black pepper to taste in a medium bowl. Pour egg batter over stuffed chiles. Sprinkle cheddar cheese evenly over eggs and chiles. Bake for 45 minutes. Serve immediately.

 Serve with salsa or a tossed green salad for a pick-up supper or with a bowl of fresh cut-up fruit for a nourishing midmorning breakfast.

Serves: 4

Cheese Grits with Bacon Bits

Loaded with cheese and bacon, these grits make a filling supper when the refrigerator is nearly bare. Or, fry up a couple of eggs and serve the grits casserole in the morning as a hearty breakfast entrée.

6 slices bacon, cut into ¼-inch pieces

1½ cups quick grits

8 tablespoons (1 stick) butter, cut into 8 pieces

8 ounces sharp cheddar cheese, shredded (3 cups)

1 tablespoon Worcestershire sauce

1¼ teaspoons Hungarian paprika, divided

½ teaspoon salt

3 eggs, beaten

Preheat oven to 325°F. Cook bacon in a medium nonstick skillet over medium-low heat until crisp. Remove with a slotted spoon and drain on paper toweling.

Cook grits according to package instructions. Stir in butter and cheese until melted. Stir in Worcestershire sauce, 1 teaspoon paprika, and salt. Add 1 tablespoon hot grits to eggs and stir to combine. Stir egg mixture and bacon into grits.

Coat a 2-quart baking dish with vegetable cooking spray. Transfer grits to baking dish. Sprinkle with remaining paprika. Bake, uncovered, for 1 hour. Serve immediately.

You can assemble this casserole up to 2 days ahead. Cover and refrigerate it until needed. Remove dish from refrigerator 15 minutes before baking. You can use regular paprika instead of the Hungarian, but it will simply add a little color and very little flavor.

Serves: 8

Santa Fe Vegetable Tortilla Soup

This hearty soup, made almost entirely from pantry items, comes together in mere minutes. It is the perfect meal to serve when the refrigerator is bare.

8 corn tortillas

Olive oil spray

1 (19-ounce) can Progresso Hearty Tomato Soup

1½ cups chicken broth

3 cups water

1 (15.25-ounce) can whole kernel corn, drained

1 (14.5-ounce) can green beans, drained and cut into 1-inch pieces

1 (14.5-ounce) can Mexican-style diced tomatoes, with juices

1 (4-ounce) can chopped green chiles, drained

1 (1-ounce) package mild taco seasoning mix

1 cup shredded Monterey Jack cheese

Preheat oven to 350°F. Cut tortillas into ½-inch strips with kitchen scissors. Place tortilla strips on 2 nonstick baking sheets. Coat strips lightly with olive oil spray. Bake for 5 minutes. Toss strips with a firm spatula. Bake for 5 minutes more. Remove tortilla strips from oven and allow them to cool.

Place tomato soup, chicken broth, water, corn, beans, tomatoes, chiles, and taco seasoning mix in a large soup pot over medium heat. Stir to combine ingredients well. Bring to a boil, uncovered. Reduce heat to low, cover, and simmer soup for 15 minutes.

Top each serving with one-eighth the tortilla strips and 2 tablespoons shredded cheese.

You can substitute tomato juice or V-8 juice for part of the water in this recipe. If you like your food very, very spicy, use the original taco seasoning rather than the mild version. Store any leftover cooled tortilla strips in a zipper bag at room temperature.

Serves: 8

Essential to any successful makeover are an arsenal of ammunition and a secret bag of tricks. In culinary circles, that means Stocking the Pantry, 'Fridge, and Freezer — the ammo in this section — as well as some innovative, unusual, or just tried-and-true rituals that transform dinner from average to amazing, mundane to meteoric — the Makeover Tips that follow.

STOCKING THE PANTRY, 'FRIDGE, AND FREEZER

Pantry

PRODUCE
bananas

garlic

onions: sweet onions like Vidalia, red onions

potatoes: new red potatoes, sweet potatoes

shallots

squash: butternut, spaghetti

tomatoes: slicing, grape, plum or Roma

BAKING SUPPLIES
Bisquick

cornstarch

Crisco

evaporated milk

extracts: vanilla, almond, coconut

flour (all-purpose)

sugar: granulated white, confectioners', light brown, dark brown

SEASONINGS AND MIXES
bread crumbs (dried): panko, Italian seasoned

broth and stock: beef, chicken, seafood, vegetable, College Inn White Wine & Herb Chicken broth

bouillon cubes: beef, vegetable, chicken

dried fruits: cranberries, apricots, raisins, golden raisins, currants

jams/jellies/marmalades: orange marmalade, red currant jelly, mango chutney

nuts and seeds: salted peanuts, honey-roasted peanuts, cashews, sesame seeds (white and black)

pepper: cracked black pepper, ground black pepper, white pepper, crushed red pepper flakes, cayenne, lemon pepper

salt: kosher or coarse salt, table salt, lemon sea salt

sauce mixes: Creamy Garlic Alfredo Sauce, Four Cheese Sauce (McCormick), ranch dip mix

spices: allspice, basil, bay leaves, caraway seeds, celery seed, chili powder, chipotle chile powder, cinnamon, citrus grill seasoning (Durkee's), cloves, coriander (ground), cream of tartar, cumin, curry powder (mild Sharwood's or Madras), dry mustard, garlic powder, lemon-dill seasoning, lemon-herb seasoning, marjoram, garlic-herb seasoning (McCormick), nutmeg, onion flakes (dried), onion powder, oregano, parsley, paprika (sweet and Hungarian), poultry seasoning, seafood seasoning, tarragon, thyme, turmeric

sun-dried tomatoes

taco seasoning mix

MISCELLANEOUS

chips (Frito's corn chips)

cocoa mix (Ghirardelli Premium Double Chocolate Hot Cocoa Mix)

corn tortillas

crackers (oyster)

flour tortillas: 6.5-inch, 8-inch, 10-inch, Mission brand Spinach-Herb Wraps

fruit-and-nut trail mix

juices: apple, apricot nectar

liquor: beer, white wine, red wine, sherry, Grand Marnier, coconut rum, Triple Sec, dry vermouth

pasta: penne, ziti, no-cook flat lasagna noodles, jumbo shells, manicotti shells, spaghetti, angel hair or capellini, fettuccine, orzo

peanut butter (creamy)

pizza crusts (Mama Mary's Gourmet Pizza Thin & Crispy Crusts)

quick grits

rice: basmati, jasmine, arborio, brown and wild rice mixture

rice noodles

shiitake mushrooms (dried)

split peas (green)

CANNED GOODS

beans: black, great northern

chicken breast (white meat in water)

chiles: mild green diced, mild green whole

coconut milk: light, regular, unsweetened

corn (whole kernel)

cranberry sauce (jellied)

green beans

olives (black sliced)

pumpkin puree

soup: cream of chicken, Progresso Hearty Tomato

tomatillos

tomato paste: plain, with basil, garlic, and oregano

tomato sauce

tomatoes: crushed or puree; diced with basil, garlic, and oregano; Mexican-style diced; petite-cut in garlic and olive oil; and stewed (with onions, celery, and green peppers, and with basil, garlic, and oregano)

JAR OR BOTTLED GOODS

Asian sweet chili sauce

barbecue sauce (smoky flavor)

basil pesto

black bean dip

capers

fish sauce

honey

hot sauce or Tabasco sauce

hoisin sauce

ketchup

mayonnaise

mint sauce

mirin

molasses

mustard: Dijon mustard, cranberry honey mustard or other fruit-flavored honey mustard, stone-ground

oils: olive, light olive, extra-virgin olive, canola, olive oil spray, vegetable oil spray, toasted sesame

oyster sauce

pasta sauce: garlic tomato, tomato and basil, marinara

plum sauce

roasted red peppers

salsa (chunky)

soy sauce

vinegars: white, red wine, white wine, rice, cider, white balsamic, raspberry

Worcestershire sauce

Freezer

BREADS

breads: whole grain, cinnamon swirl, Italian, naan, artisan, petite round white

buns and rolls: 3-inch rolls or Walmart White Dollar Rolls, sesame seed, Kaiser, knot rolls

Real New York Pizza Dough

STAPLE INGREDIENTS

bread crumbs, fresh *(see Makeover Tips section)*

butter *(see Makeover Tips section)*

cheese (shredded, crumbled): blue, goat, Swiss, Monterey Jack, sharp cheddar, 4-Cheese Italian, 4-Cheese Mexican blend, mozzarella

citrus zest: orange, lime, lemon *(See Makeover Tips section.)*

fruits: sliced peaches, sliced mangoes

herbs: snipped flat-leaf parsley, basil, rosemary, cilantro, chives, thyme, oregano, mint, curly parsley, dill *(see Makeover Tips section)*

juices: orange juice concentrate, fresh lemon, lime, orange *(see Makeover Tips section)*

nuts: sliced almonds, pine nuts, pecans *(see Makeover Tips section)*

pie crusts: deep dish in foil pan, Pillsbury 9-inch Ready Crusts

potatoes (country-style hash brown potatoes)

MEAT, SEAFOOD, AND POULTRY

beef: lean ground, sirloin steak cut 1½ inches thick, flank steak

chicken: boneless, skinless breasts; whole fryers

ducks

ham (spiral)

lamb (boneless leg)

pork: boneless loin roast, boneless pork chops, pork tenderloins

pork sausage (Jimmy Dean's Hot Pork Sausage)

shrimp (uncooked, shell on): 10/15s, 16/20s, 51/60s

turkey: whole, breast

Refrigerator

PRODUCE

apples (sweet-tart)

asparagus

bean sprouts

bell peppers: red, orange, yellow, green

broccoli slaw

carrots: baby, petite baby, shredded, whole

celery

chile peppers (jalapeño)

citrus: oranges, lemons, limes

cranberries

cucumber (English)

grapes (red)

jicama

juices: orange, lemon, lime (see *Makeover Tips section*)

leafy greens: baby spinach, iceberg lettuce, romaine lettuce hearts, Boston or bibb lettuce, mixed baby greens, arugula

mushrooms (fresh): white button, baby bella

peaches

pears

pineapple

scallions

snow pea pods

sweet corn

Yukon Gold potatoes (These potatoes have a higher sugar content than other potatoes. Store them in a paper bag or perforated plastic bag in crisper drawer of refrigerator.)

zucchini

DAIRY

butter: salted, unsalted

cheese (chunk): mozzarella, sharp cheddar, pepper jack, Brie, cheddar-jack, Swiss, Monterey Jack, Gruyère

cheese (sliced): Swiss

cream cheese: whipped cream cheese, chive and onion spread

dill dip

eggs (large)

eggnog

half-and-half

heavy whipping cream

margarine

milk: whole, skim

Parmesan cheese (grated)

ricotta cheese

sour cream

yogurt (plain)

MEAT, SEAFOOD, AND POULTRY

bacon

fish: wild Alaskan sockeye salmon, swordfish cut 1½ inches thick, yellowfin tuna steaks cut 1 inch thick

rotisserie chicken (supermarket delicatessen)

MISCELLANEOUS

egg roll wrappers (6-inch-square)

guacamole

herb pastes: garlic, gingerroot

horseradish (prepared)

Pillsbury Big & Buttery Crescent Rolls

salsa (mild tomato, mango)

Equipment and Supplies

- **Special bakeware:** You'll need four ¾-cup round ramekins for the Crusty Baskets (Duck-Noodle Salad); an 8-inch diameter, 4-inch deep round baking dish for Potato, Onion, and Bacon Bake; a shallow 10-inch round baking dish for Spaghetti Squash Primavera; a 2-quart baking dish for Cheese Grits and for Roasted Butternut Squash-Sweet Potato Pesto-Mash; and a 10-inch fluted tart pan with loose bottom for Savory Shrimp Tart. Fancy Schmancy Meatloaf requires a molded nonstick loaf pan, such as the Nordic Ware Fancy Bundt Loaf Pan.

- **Aluminum baking pans:** Use a large roasting pan for the Roast Duck and Grill-roasted Turkey; Hefty brand 1½-quart foil casserole pans for Baked Chicken Ziti; and 8x8x1½-inch pan for Breakfast Bread Pudding. Assemble Spicy Meat Loaf–Mushroom Lasagna in a 13x10x4-inch-deep aluminum lasagna pan.

- **Other pans you'll need:** Broiler pan, nonstick skillets and saucepans (small, medium, large), soup pot, pizza pan, pizza stone, wok or stir-fry pan, baking sheets, metal roasting rack, deep-dish pie plate, baking pans (7x11-inch, 10x13-inch, 8x8-inch, 6x9-inch).

- **Grilling equipment:** You'll need metal skewers for the Lemon-Mint Chicken Kabobs and the Barbecued Jumbo Shrimp. The seafood will stay in place better if metal skewers have flat shafts instead of round. Beer Can Chicken requires two ChickCan racks.

- **Small appliances:** You'll need a slow cooker for the Red Currant Glazed Corned Beef. Many of the recipes call for a blender, food processor, electric mixer, or microwave oven.

- **Cooking oil pump sprayer:** Misto is a popular brand found at most stores that sell kitchen supplies. Light olive oil or canola oil works best in the sprayer. Using real cooking oil is more economical, allows for a more even and controllable spray, and is free of the chemicals commonly found in commercial aerosol cooking sprays.

- **Two sets of measuring cups:** You need one set of measuring cups for liquids (1-cup, 2-cup, and/or 4-cup glass or plastic calibrated in ounces) and one set for measuring dry ingredients (1 cup, ½ cup, ⅓ cup, ¼ cup). Level dry ingredients with a knife.

- **Parchment paper:** You can substitute butcher paper or waxed paper for parchment paper when flash-freezing items, but don't make such a substitution when baking. You do not have to grease a baking sheet if you line it with parchment paper.

- **Microplane grater:** One of a cook's best investments is an ultra-sharp microplane grater, available at most stores that sell kitchenware (about $15). You can grate lemon, lime, or orange peel in mere seconds. You can finely grate gingerroot, garlic, onion, or even chocolate.

- **Mini muffin pans:** Mini muffin pans have twenty-four 2-inch cups, each holding about 1 ounce. You'll need the mini muffin pan for the Mini Ham Popovers.

- **Storage Items:** Plastic wrap, aluminum foil, parchment paper, freezer-weight zipper bags, and covered plastic containers in various sizes.

MAKEOVER TIPS

- You'll never have to mince garlic or grate gingerroot again when you use pastes from Gourmet Gardens (in the produce section of your supermarket). The finely ground herb pastes last for months and eliminate prep time mincing, chopping, and snipping. I always keep the garlic and gingerroot pastes in my refrigerator, but the company also makes red chili pepper, cilantro, basil, and lemongrass pastes as well. Cost is about 19 cents a tablespoon. The pastes are real time savers.

- One of the secrets to a flavorful culinary makeover is a well-stocked spice stash. Mine actually inhabits several shelves of my pantry. Spices, however, can be expensive, especially when you may use the seasonings infrequently. I buy my spices from www.penzeys.com. The company sells an exceptionally wide range of fresh spices in small quantities at reasonable prices. They have retail stores in only a handful of cities in the U.S., but they offer a complete color catalog as well as a great Web site for ordering over the Internet.

- The other essential flavor weapon in my arsenal is a freezer full of fresh herbs, snipped and flash-frozen. I buy bundles of fresh herbs when they are inexpensive and plentiful in the summer season: curly and flat-leaf parsley, basil, rosemary, cilantro, chives, thyme, oregano, mint, dill. I turn on the television, grab a pair of kitchen scissors, and snip the herbs (rinsed and spun dry) into a bowl as I watch the news or a movie. Then I transfer the herbs to individual zipper bags, label, and freeze them. Frozen herbs will keep in the freezer for a year, are easy to measure, and add a jolt of flavor freshness that dried herbs simply can't muster. (If you must resort to using dried herbs, use one-third to one-half the amount of fresh herbs, depending upon the age of the dried herbs. Dried herbs lose their potency over time.)

- I find that fresh bread crumbs work much better in a lot of recipes than dried crumbs. I put my odds and ends of bread in the food processor (don't worry if they are different types of breads), process them until they are fine-grained, then transfer them to a freezer-weight zipper bag that I keep in the freezer. The bread crumbs will keep up to a year.

- Storing buns and rolls in the freezer guarantees you'll have what you'll need for a quick makeover sandwich. Often, however, frozen bread and rolls get freezer-burned and turn dry and tasteless. I have found that wrapping individual buns and rolls in plastic wrap before freezing and then placing them in a freezer-weight zipper bag, keeps them bakery-fresh once defrosted.

- The addition of dried fruits or chopped nuts adds a flavor boost to lots of dishes. While dried fruits can be kept almost indefinitely in the pantry, only a few roasted nuts, like peanuts and cashews, should be stored this way. I keep bags of chopped walnuts, pecans, macadamia nuts, pistachios, pine nuts, and sliced almonds in my freezer so they don't become rancid. Place them in a small nonstick skillet over low heat and dry-toast them before adding them to salads or sprinkling them over cooked food as a garnish. If you are using them in a recipe, you can use them frozen.

- Fresh citrus juices and grated peel are essential elements in my cooking. My supermarket —

and probably yours too — sells bags of "overripe" oranges, limes, and lemons for a fraction of the price usually charged for these expensive fruits. (A mere eighty-nine cents usually nets me six or seven lemons.) If the peel is still unblemished, I grate the citrus with a microplaner (see Equipment and Supplies list) and then freeze the zest in a labeled zipper bag. I juice the citrus and freeze it in small plastic containers. I also keep small bottles of lemon juice and lime juice in the refrigerator at all times. If a recipe calls for a tablespoon of fresh lemon juice, it is at my fingertips.

- Many recipes call for just a tablespoon of tomato paste or a quarter cup of tomato sauce or even a small amount of pesto. I wrap the unused portion of tomato paste in plastic wrap, forming a cigar-shaped roll, and freeze it. When I need another tablespoon of paste, I simply unroll the plastic wrap and cut off what I need with a sharp paring knife. I freeze extra tomato sauce and pesto in an ice cube tray and store the cubes in labeled zipper bags. I store unused chicken, beef, and vegetable broth in ½-cup plastic containers in the freezer. They defrost in the microwave in seconds. Waste not, want not!

- One of the keys to a successful culinary makeover is to keep the handful of ingredients essential to creating ethnic dishes in your pantry arsenal. I favor the small protein–big flavor approach of the Asian and Mexican cultures. By adding rice or veggies, they make a little go a long, long way! For Asian dishes — Chinese, Thai, Japanese, Indonesian — stock Asian sweet chili sauce, fish sauce, hoisin sauce, plum sauce, oyster sauce, soy sauce, mirin (Japanese sweet cooking wine), rice vinegar, toasted sesame oil, and coconut milk. For Mexican or Spanish food, keep an array of corn and flour tortillas on hand, as well as mild and hot chiles, salsa, black beans, tomatillos, hot sauce, frozen guacamole, and frozen shredded cheese. With these staples plus a fully stocked spice stash and a freezer full of herbs, I am always amazed at how easily my taste buds can trot the globe.

- I think takeout pizza tastes like cardboard, so I love making my own. I don't take the time to make authentic pizza dough, instead keeping Mama Mary's, Boboli, or other prepared crusts and naan bread (flatbread) in the pantry. While the crust may not quite taste like it came from Italy, it doesn't matter when loaded with the array of toppings I keep in my arsenal. I store 4-ounce portions of raw hot sausage, handfuls of smoked pepperoni, and leftover cooked bits of chicken, beef, and shrimp in freezer-weight zipper bags in the freezer along with bags of shredded mozzarella. They all defrost in seconds, and along with some bottled marinara sauce, pine nuts, raisins, and a potpourri of chopped veggies, it is pizza my way.

- Homemade soup is far superior to the canned varieties, both in taste and nutritional values, and is a great venue for a makeover meal. But a pot full of soup can last for days. Who wants to eat the same soup every day for a week? Here is the quick, easy answer: Freeze extra soup and chili in maxi muffin tins. Each muffin cup holds 1 cup. Pop frozen soup out of the muffin cups and store in labeled freezer-weight zipper bags in the freezer. When you want a cup of soup, place a frozen soup block in a microwave-safe bowl, then defrost and reheat it. This is also a convenient way to take lunch to work: Place a block of soup in a covered microwave-safe container. Take it to work with you and allow the soup to defrost at room temperature all morning. By lunchtime, the soup will be defrosted and you can reheat it in the microwave. Easy, tasty, and inexpensive!

- Butter freezes very well. I always buy several pounds when I find it on sale and keep it on hand in the freezer, defrosting and using it stick by stick. Butter comes salted and unsalted. When butter is called for in the recipes in this book, use salted butter. (I indicate when unsalted butter is required, usually in baking.) Salt is added as a preservative, which is not needed as long as you keep your butter refrigerated, so if all you have is unsalted butter, add 1/4 teaspoon salt per ½ cup butter when salted butter is indicated.

- I always like to use sweet onions, like Vidalia or Walla Walla in all my recipes. These onions have a higher sugar content than Spanish yellow onions, so they are not as strong-tasting and have a mild, sweet flavor. Because of the higher sugar content, however, they don't store as long as other onions. Keep them refrigerated and buy only the amount you'd use within two weeks time. On the other hand, shallots — a distant cousin of the onion — store well for months in the refrigerator. Very important in most cuisines around the world, shallots have a mild flavor with a hint of garlic. If a recipe calls for shallots and you don't have them, use an equal amount of chopped onions and add a finely minced clove of garlic.

- A staple in many cultures and cuisines, rice is a great medium with which to create a culinary makeover. I always keep three distinctly different kinds on hand in my pantry: basmati, jasmine, and arborio. Basmati rice — a long-grain rice grown in India and Pakistan — is fluffy and flavorful with a distinctive aroma. Jasmine rice is a long-grain Thai rice with a fragrant, nutty aroma that partners well when cooked with coconut milk. Arborio rice is short-grained with a high starch content. The rice required in making a good risotto, arborio has a creamy, chewy consistency that absorbs flavors well. Cooked basmati and jasmine rices freeze very well, so I always make much more than I need at the moment and use it in a potpourri of other dishes at a later date.

- When all else fails and the cupboard is bare, one of the most versatile makeover artists is the simple egg. Look for the freshest eggs possible at your supermarket. How do you tell if the eggs are fresh? Examine the data stamped on the carton! Two dates are printed on egg cartons: One is the "sell by" date. The other is a 9-digit number called the Julian date, the last three numbers of which indicate the day of the year the eggs were packed. For instance, 097 would be April 7, the 97th day of the year. For the eggs to be fresh, the "sell by" date should be no more than 30 days after the Julian date and preferably as close to the Julian date as possible.

TABLE OF EQUIVALENTS

Some of the conversions in these lists have been slightly rounded for measuring convenience.

VOLUME:

U.S.	metric
¼ teaspoon	1.25 milliliters
½ teaspoon	2.5 milliliters
¾ teaspoon	3.75 milliliters
1 teaspoon	5 milliliters
1 tablespoon (3 teaspoons)	15 milliliters
2 tablespoons	30 milliliters
3 tablespoons	45 milliliters
1 fluid ounce (2 tablespoons)	30 milliliters
¼ cup	60 milliliters
⅓ cup	80 milliliters
½ cup	120 milliliters
⅔ cup	160 milliliters
1 cup	240 milliliters
2 cups (1 pint)	480 milliliters
4 cups (1 quart or 32 ounces)	960 milliliters
1 gallon (4 quarts)	3.8 liters

OVEN TEMPERATURE:

fahrenheit	celsius
250	120
275	140
300	150
325	160
350	180
375	190
400	200
425	220
450	230
475	240
500	260

WEIGHT:

U.S.	metric
1 ounce (by weight)	28 grams
1 pound	448 grams
2.2 pounds	1 kilogram

LENGTH:

U.S.	metric
⅛ inch	3 millimeters
¼ inch	6 millimeters
½ inch	12 millimeters
1 inch	2.5 centimeters

Acknowledgments

Here I go again quoting the Beatles, just as I have for the past five books I have written. The four lads sang: "I get by with a little help from my friends!" and it was especially true in the creation of *Leftover Makeovers*.

My enduring gratitude goes to my most patient critic and chief guinea pig, my husband, Bob, and to my most loyal taste testers — Vivienne and Frank Afshari, Bill and Sue Hendrick, Ola Lilley, and Randy and Susie Williams. Your courage was admirable and your input invaluable. And to those folks who augmented the scores of recipes I developed by sharing some of their personal favorites: Rita Cencich, Shirley Grahek, Linda McGaan, Meg Nelson, Brian Shearer, Louise Skidmore, and Susie Williams — thank you, thank you, thank you!

To the person who keeps me in the kitchen and has made this cookbook series possible, Megan Hiller at Sellers Publishing, thanks for believing in me yet again. I so enjoy working with you.

And of course, along with my hubby, thanks to my family: the Rochester Shearers — Brian, Lisa, Bethany, Bobby, and Leia; the Raleigh Wingenbachs — Kristen, John, Ashleigh, Christopher, and Nicholas; and the Florida golden girls — mother June Harbort and aunt Fern Miller. Always hungry and game to try anything, you all helped make this book possible.